A Blessed and Guided Life

AN AUTOBIOGRAPHY

From the Streets of Brooklyn to ...

Robert Giarraffa

Copyrighted Material

A Blessed and Guided Life
Copyright © 2020 by Robert Giarraffa. All Rights Reserved.
Revised January 2022.

No part of this publication may be reproduced, stored in a retrieval system or transmitted, in any form or by any means—electronic, mechanical, photocopying, recording or otherwise—without prior written permission from the publisher, except for the inclusion of brief quotations in a review.

For information about this title or to order other books and/or electronic media, contact the publisher:
Datar Publishing
P.O. Box 333 Ironia, NJ 07845
nhfs1@aol.com

ISBN: 978-1-7337989-0-7 (Hardcover)
       978-1-7337989-2-1 (Softcover)
       978-1-7337989-1-4 (eBook)

Printed in the United States of America

Cover and Interior design: 1106 Design

*This book is dedicated to our earthly treasures:
Gabriella, Sophia, Domenick, Cesare, and Siena.*

Table of Contents

Preface ix

Pre-Me (My Family History) I
- My Father 1
- My Mother 4

Becoming Me 9
- My Birth 9
- Childhood 10
- Elementary School 18
- High School 1960 to 1964 21
- College 1964 to 1968 29
- National Guard 1969 to 1975 34
- Hair Challenged 43

Me as Me (My Career) 45
- Warner Lambert 45
- Financial Advisor Beginnings 62
- Job Change 66
- Appointment with Marlene 1984 70
- TFS Conventions 1985 to 2009 78

Me as We (Married Life) 83
- Meeting Savia 85
- My First Official Date 87
- Savia 90
- The Beginning of Our Life Together. 92
  46 Dafrack Drive 1971 to 1973
- Our First House. 93
  70 Sanford Drive 1973 to 1990
- Young and Fearless. 96
  Extra Income
- Making New Friends 100
  Hawaii Trip 1975
- The Right People for the Job? 103
  Moving the Plane 1987
- Houseboat Hell. 112
  Rideau Lakes 1988
- The Eye Venture. 119
  Mom's Eyes 1990
- Talk About Risk! 120
  Is This Our Dream House?
- Part of History. 125
  Garth Brooks Concert 1997
- Attitude Is Everything 127
  Joey's Baseball Game
- From Physical to Spiritual. 129
  Alabama Trip 2015
- A Kid Again 135
  Grandmasters Softball 1997 to 2020+

- The Move of a Lifetime 138
    Mom at 92
- Mohonk Adventure 155
    A Close Call
- From Bikes to Buses..................... 157
    Bermuda Trip 2018
- A Holiday to Remember.................. 164
    It Was Up to Us 2020
- An Extraordinary Trip to the Post Office...... 166
    Angels at Work
- Around the Town....................... 171
    Community Service
    Unintended Consequences
- Who Am I?............................ 173
    Names

Mini-Me 177
- Children............................. 177
- Grandchildren 183
    - Driving Gabriella and Sophia to School .. 184
    - The Visit............................ 186
    - Notes to Grandchildren 191

Me for Thee (My Philosophy and Legacy) 193
- Family Story Book 193
- Traditions............................ 194
    - Family Vacations.................... 194
    - Italy............................... 195
    - Traveling Salesman...................200
    - Bedtime Lullaby.....................202

- Easter-Egg Hunt 204
- Seating Arrangements. 206
- Making Struffoli. 206
- Ending. 209

Acknowledgments 213

About the Author 215

Preface

It has been said that there are more stars in the sky than grains of sand on all the beaches of the world. This can give you a faint glimmer of how big our universe is and how small we are. So why am I writing a story of my life? Isn't my life or any life insignificant? Not at all. We are all unique individuals, with a physical, emotional, intellectual, and a spiritual life. A spark of divinity was created within each life. Some of us are exceptional or geniuses in math, others in the arts, others in compassion, or in teaching, and so on. It is up to us to uncover this talent and to be the best version of ourselves. Once we determine our gift(s) and the reason we are here, the happier we will be, and the more we can contribute to the world. As you read these stories, you may come across something that can help you in your life. They might contain a lesson that resonates with you. You may learn something from either my good example or my bad example. Perhaps this book will just be entertaining, or it may inspire you to write your own story. Your experiences and knowledge are part of what you leave for future generations. All our knowledge comes from standing on the shoulders of people who came before us.

A Blessed and Guided Life

If you want to get to know about Robert Giarraffa, you have come to the right place. This is the only authoritative book on the subject. You may be one of my children or grandchildren, or someone else. Over these pages, you will learn about my life and my experiences; perhaps you'll see something of yourself in these stories. Names have *not* been changed to protect the innocent. As we get older, we accumulate memories and stories that we don't want to lose. This is my attempt to preserve those stories. Although this is about my life, it relies heavily on shared experiences with my family. Without them, I would not have a life.

Pre-Me (My Family History)
Where it all started — Mom and Dad

My father, Domenick, was born on February 15, 1919. He had five brothers and three sisters. When he was young, his father was out of work for a short time, and his mom was sick. The children had to stay at St. John's Orphanage Home for two months and were forced to eat oatmeal every day, which he disliked. During the rest of his life, just the smell of oatmeal repulsed him and brought him back to the home. I think sharing the experience together in the orphanage brought his brothers and sisters even closer together. You could tell they loved one another and loved life. In 1936, when he was 19, there was an epidemic of pneumonia. One day, when he wasn't feeling well, his brother Iggy and his fiancée Amelia came to visit him. Amelia noticed that he was gagging. She lifted his head up, and a gush of blood came out. He was rushed to the hospital and was in a coma for two months. Amelia saved his life. When he awoke, he had to learn to walk again. He went from a wheelchair to using a cane before he could walk again. This episode left him with phlebitis, which he learned to cope with — or should I say "ignore."

Although many of his brothers served in Europe, Dad was inducted into the Army as a supply clerk in the Signal Corps and served at Camp Crowder, Missouri, from November 1942 until he was discharged in September of 1943.

When I was 11 years old, my Dad took me to the movies. It was a five block walk to the Benson Theatre, which he pronounced *thee-ate-tur*, to see *The Vikings*. That was the only time we went to the movies together. To this day, it is still one of my favorite movies, because it connects me to him.

When I was young, I asked my father a question. "Dad, did you ever regret that you were not a successful, important person?" Remember, I was young at the time. He said, "If you do everything the best that you can, you *are* successful and important." Everything he did was to perfection. There were no shortcuts and no time limitations. He kept working at it until it met his standards, which far exceeded what was simply necessary.

My father was always happy and cheerful — and why not? He considered himself to have a blessed life. As a devoted husband and father, he did whatever was needed to provide for his family. For several years, he held two full-time jobs, a part-time job, and went to Radio School, all at the same time. He worked for Dromedary, a division of Hills Brothers, a dried-fruit-and-nut company, and would bring home chunks of citrus fruit for us. He cleaned buses for the city of New York. In 1961, he worked as a gardener on Shore Road in Brooklyn. When Dad worked nights, I would play outside during the day, but quietly, since Dad was sleeping so he could be rested for his night job. Sometimes Mom and I would

Pre-Me (My Family History)

stay up making puzzles until he arrived home at 2:15 a.m. He would have a glass of milk and some Ritz crackers before going to bed. He retired at age 57.

He had a wonderful, caring, loving wife, wonderful children and grandchildren, brothers, sisters, and friends who loved him. He had so much love in him that sometimes it was hard for him to contain it. He cried often. He spoke to everyone who crossed his path. Strangers' children would make drawings for him.

In Dad's view, everyone should love everyone else.

We were at church one Sunday, and I noticed tears in my father's eyes when the priest said, "Peace be with you." I asked him if there was something wrong. My father said, "I don't think that there will ever be world peace." That is how sensitive and loving he was.

I never heard him say anything negative about anyone. He didn't know how to curse or get angry.

When I was about 30 years old, my daughter did something that made me angry. I don't remember what it was. I didn't know how to act. I had to ask my wife, Savia, how to display anger. What body language do I use? What facial expression is appropriate? I didn't know. I realized that I had never seen my role model, my father, get angry. All he knew was love.

He also had at least three special superpowers. First, he could swallow pills without water. He said all you needed was the right timing. Second, once we noticed him tripping. He fell to the ground, rolled on his back, and, in one continuous motion, got up and continued walking as if nothing had happened. Third, several times he was sitting at a table, and a glass of liquid, sometimes hot, would spill in his direction.

He would spring back from the table as if he were a pilot in an ejection seat. He always escaped.

I must say, jokingly, that I am not sure if my father directly experienced life. His eyes were always behind a video camera, taking movies. He recorded everyone and everything that crossed his path. Therefore, I don't need to have memories: they are recorded for me. What a wonderful legacy he left us.

Dad had a stroke on April 15, 2003, resulting in aphasia, an inability to communicate or formulate language.

On September 14, he was at my daughter Daria's wedding and visited with all his friends and relatives. It was a wonderful wedding and reunion, and, even though he could not speak, we knew he was happy.

The weekend before he died, we went apple picking, went on a hayride and then to a Knights of Columbus Italian Dinner Dance at our church St. Lawrence Church, in Chester. It was one of the most joyful days in our lives.

I thank God for all the years we had together. On November 6, 2003, he moved on to the Next Phase of Life. I have it from a reliable source that he is happy, energetic, and curious, as always, to see who he could help with their gardening.

My mother, Matilda, known as "Tillie," was born on June 8, 1922. She was the fifth of seven children; she had three brothers and three sisters and lived at 44 Strong Place in Brooklyn. Her maiden name was Ospitale. The family story says the name came about because her great-grandfather was left at the doorstep of a hospital when he was an infant. He was then given the name "Ospitale," which means "hospital" in Italian.

Pre-Me (My Family History)

Mom and Dad's 50th Anniversary

When Mom was 16, her friend Ann asked her to cut school and go on a boat ride with her and her boyfriend Ralph Esposito to Bear Mountain in upstate New York. This is where she first met my father. The four of them remained lifelong friends. Mom didn't realize that the person who delivered ice to their house was my father. He would deliver early in the morning while she was still asleep. Mom and Dad were married at St. Stephen's Church and had their wedding reception at Gargiulo's in Coney Island, Brooklyn, on September 3, 1944. They rented an apartment at 154 Carroll Street. In 1951, Mom and Dad bought a house together with Mom's sister Rose and her husband Ralph at 2328 83rd Street in Brooklyn, where Mom lived with two of her sisters and their families for most of her life.

I believe one of the reasons we are here is to conquer our fears. I think Mom had that under control. She was the first woman President of the American Legion, not afraid to be a leader. Since both her children got married and moved to New Jersey, she said that she did not see her children often enough, so, at age 50, she learned to drive so she could see us more often. *Who does that?*

Mom was the crossing guard at St. Mary's School for 15 years. She crossed most of Bensonhurst. She knew the names of everyone — the children *and* their parents. When she was 90, more than 40 years after being a crossing guard, she was so surprised and happy that many of the children she'd crossed still recognized and remembered her. "Hey Tillie! How you doin?", yelling out of a passing car window while she walked down the street.

Mom volunteered for the Democratic Party, going door to door for support and working at the election booth. She knew all the politicians in Brooklyn. She was active at church and a member of the Rosary Society.

Because of everyone she knew and her pleasant personality, we gave her the title "Miss Bensonhurst."

Her sense of humor was legendary. She loved jokes, especially off-color jokes, although they had nothing to do with "color." Friends and family would constantly send her jokes, resulting in a library-worthy collection.

Based upon the average human life span, when you see someone here for 93 years, you get to feel like they will always be here. Unfortunately, that is not the case.

Becoming Me (My Birth, Childhood, and School Years)

My Birth

I was born at a very early age. I entered the world feet first, ahead of schedule, on Friday, January 3, 1947, at 7:29 p.m. My mother was nauseous during most of her pregnancy with me. I was born premature and weighed only about 3½ pounds. Later in life, my father would place a five-pound bag of sugar in his hand and say to me, "You were a little more than one-half the size of this bag." When you are Catholic and nearing the end of your life, you are given what is called "Last Rites." This prepares you for the next life. My mother and I were doing so poorly when I was born that we *both* received Last Rites. Fortunately, we made it through.

Back then, premature babies were placed in an incubator with special lights to keep them warm and protect them from jaundice. It was discovered later that there were side effects to this light, including blindness. Luckily, the incubator I was placed in did not have lights. Since I was born prematurely, I always wondered if there were some organs or body parts in me that did not have time to fully develop. I'd picture going to the hospital for some procedure, and when the surgeon opened me up, he would say, "Where is the (fill in the missing body part)?" Mom said they named me "Robert" after a popular movie star of the time, Robert Ryan.

Three years later, on May 5, 1950, my sister Loretta was born. After the first experience with me, it's surprising that there was a second child. My parents must have been very brave and/or crazy.

My Childhood

The earliest memory I have is walking under the kitchen table when we lived on 154 Carroll Street in Brooklyn. In 1951, my Uncle Ralph found a house in the Bensonhurst section of Brooklyn, a mile from the water. My parents lived on the ground floor; mom's sister and her husband — Aunt Rose and Uncle Ralph and their daughter Rose (Posey) lived on the second floor; mom's other sister — Aunt Jo and her two sons, Johnny and Bernie, lived on the top floor of 2328 83rd Street, in Brooklyn.

Each block in Brooklyn was like its own island. Everyone knew each other, and all the kids played together based on their age group. It seemed that each year, everyone was somehow aware when it was time to ride your bike or put on your roller skates or start the stickball season. There was a rhythm to the activities. Each season had its own activities. Summer was stickball, stoop ball, and home-run derby; fall was roller skating and polynose fun; winter was snowball fights and snow forts; spring was bike riding. There were other activities like Ring-a-levio, Red Light Green Light, Skellies, Bottle Cap Wars, Hockey, making peach rings, wax-candle burning,

Strat-o-matic, and flipping baseball cards. The girls had their own schedule of activities.

I designed the name TABER for my group of immediate friends.

> T — Tommy Spoleti
>
> A — Andy Accera
>
> B — Bobby Giarraffa
>
> E — Eddie _____
>
> R — Roger Lelack

Let me review some of the games we played at that time.

Home Run Derby would be played with a Wiffle ball and Wiffle bat. We didn't realize at the time that all Wiffle balls and bats in the world are made at one company in Connecticut. The man who started the company said they gave up playing with a regular ball because there were not enough players for two teams, not enough space for a field, and too many broken windows. He worked as a perfume-company rep and used the sample packaging the bottles were in until he came up with the current design. It hasn't changed in 50 years.

We would stand in front of the steps — we called that "the stoop" — and try to hit the ball over the fence. We lost so many Wiffle balls in the neighbor's yard across the street that we resorted to using a wad of aluminum foil as the ball. As a result, most of our neighbor's gutters were filled with aluminum foil. We thought we were doing them a favor since we did not need to go into their yards to recover a ball.

Stoop Ball used a pink Spaulding Rubber Ball. You would stand about 15 to 20 feet from the stoop and throw the ball against the steps. One bounce back to you would be 5 points, back to you with no bounces would earn 10 points, and back to you off the point of a step would be 100 points. This game also kept us occupied for hours.

Skellies was played with soda-bottle caps. We would draw a rectangle on the street pavement with six boxes in it, each representing a different value. From a distance away, you would hit a bottle cap with your fingers and try to get it into the box. The problem was that the bottle caps glided better when they were filled with asphalt from the street. We would dig the bottle cap into the street until it was filled with asphalt. Every few years, city trucks would come by and repave our street. Sounds like an expensive game.

Each kid would save the soda bottle caps in a box. During the summer, we would assemble our armies — Cokes against Pepsi, or Ginger Ale against Root Beer. Each bottle cap would be aligned face down. We would knock the two caps together until one turned over and was declared dead. We spent hours playing **Bottle Cap Wars.**

Stickball was the most popular ball game. During the summer, we would play from morning to night, with a short break for lunch. We would play to exhaustion. We used a rubber ball and a wooden broomstick. If you hit the ball a distance of two manhole covers, that was a home run. Wherever the ball was hit, you made your best effort to catch it. We were so focused on the ball that it didn't matter if you ran into a parked car in your attempt to "save the game." Several times a year, in an attempt to catch the ball, I would seriously sprain my ankle. Half my foot would land on the sidewalk curb and the other half on the street. When this happened, it would feel like I'd been hit in the ankle with a lightning bolt. I could see only in black and white. I'd spend weeks on the couch with my leg elevated. It was fun. My Aunt Jo, who lived on the third floor of our house, would call my cousins, Johnny and Bernie, for lunch with a special, high-pitched whistle. Fortunately, I could imitate her call perfectly and did so many times to trick my cousins.

Hockey was the game of choice for the colder weather. You would put your skates on over your shoes by fastening them with a skate key. If the process wasn't done correctly, the skates would not stay on very long. Eddie lived across the street and would always be the last one to put on his skates. About every fifth time Eddie had completed the laborious skate-installation process, his mother would call, "Eddie, come and throw out the garbage." Those were the only words we ever heard her speak. We all stood around waiting for Eddie to put on his skates a second time. Half an hour later, we were ready to play.

In the fall, the maple trees would drop their seeds. They would fall like helicopters. We called these polynoses. They had many uses. You could open up the middle and put it on your nose; you could blow them through straws, hitting whatever target you wanted; you could put them in a rubber band and use it as a slingshot.

Around Halloween, we would go down into Eddie's basement, melt **candles** on our hands, and experience the feeling of burning and then the cracking of dry wax when it had solidified. That was a little strange.

When a neighbor would throw out carpet or linoleum, we would cut it into small squares and nail together a long piece of wood to a short, 45-degree-angle piece of wood. You would attach a nail on one end and a clothespin on the other, add a rubber band, and you had a **carpet gun.**

Let's say you wanted to give a girl a ring, but you were a kid and had no money or brains! I came up with a solution. You would start with a peach pit. You'd place it on the asphalt street, put your shoe over it, and drag it up and down the street until it was worn down. Then you'd turn it over and drag the other side of the pit under your shoe until that was worn down. If you sanded down the middle, you had a really inexpensive wooden **Peach Pit Ring.**

The next activity required a long string, two paper cups, and a wax candle. The recipe was to cover the string with the wax, place a small hole in the bottom middle of each paper cup, thread the string through the two cups so that the bottoms of the cups would be together, and tie a knot on both ends of the string. When one person would hold their cup to their ear with the string taut, you could hear the other speak. This was our archaic version of **the telephone.** We actually ran a string from the third floor of my house to the third floor of the house across the street and could hear each other talk.

Strat-o-matic was a baseball game based upon the real-life probability of each batter to get a single, double, triple, home run, steal a base, or strike out. This was integrated with the pitchers' real-life probabilities. Every kid on the block had a team for the entire make-believe season. We kept record books for each player as well as team statistics. Each season, a schedule was created, and there were home and away games. Many, many hours were consumed by this game. My cousin John and I believe that the organizational skills, record keeping, and strategies we learned from this game assisted us in our future careers. After more than 50 years, I still have the game nicely preserved in the basement.

You may have noticed that, except for Strat-o-matic, many of the games consisted of everyday items like broomsticks, bottle caps, "polynoses," old carpeting, peach pits, string — and tons of imagination and creativity, something I think kids are lacking today.

As a child, I was a very picky eater. It was not easy for Mom to get a good meal into me, so she devised a plan of action. Every time I finished my meal, Mom would attach a flag to the clothesline in the backyard and display it in the middle of the yard. This was the signal to the neighborhood that Bobby had eaten his meal. This was supposed to be an incentive. I don't remember if it worked.

Because I slept on my stomach with my feet pointing to the corners of the room, my feet would go out in a 45° angle instead of parallel to each other when I walked. The doctor suggested that my mother tie a towel around my waist with the knot on my stomach. That stopped me from sleeping on my stomach. Also, I should practice walking along the curb with one foot in front of the other. This helped somewhat.

Speaking of curbs, we had a fox terrier dog named Chippy. He got his name because we noticed that he would go to the curb part of the sidewalk and try to chip a piece off with his teeth.

He also had a strange quirk of letting anyone into the house — not such a great guard dog. Getting out of the house was a different story. He would grab your pants or dress and not let you out. He also liked to go up the skirts of nuns who often visited. Our kitchen floor was made of linoleum, which was a great sliding material. Mom always told me not to slide since I might fall and get hurt. She was right. I did fall, but fortunately or unfortunately, Chippy broke my fall. He sprained all four legs and was in a cast for weeks. Sorry, Chippy.

Since Dad was one of nine siblings and Mom was one of seven, we had plenty of aunts, uncles, and cousins who were a constant presence in our home. Since Mom and Dad didn't drive, most visits were at our house. It was an active family life, always surrounded by relatives. During holidays, the entire family was together, and my father took the home movies to capture every event. My Uncle Ralph would often drive us to Long Island to visit my mother's sister Mary and her husband Sal Bertino, city folk who bought a farm in Smithtown, Long Island, where he raised and sold chickens and eggs. We would go to the farm, where we would help him candle eggs. That means put a candle behind the egg and see if it was fertilized — contained a baby chicken. My cousin Anthony and I were not old enough to have an entire beer by ourselves, so, instead, we split several beers.

There were two family trips I can remember during this period. The entire "house family" went to a resort in the Adirondacks called Roxmor Inn. There was beautiful scenery, a swimming pool, outdoor barbecues, and jumping rope. It was a relaxing time, and it was wonderful to see all the adults and children enjoying themselves, without the everyday chores and worries.

The house relatives went on a family trip to Niagara Falls. I still can't imagine how, but Uncle Ralph, being the only driver, drove us. There was Uncle Ralph, Aunt Rose, Aunt Jo, Mom, Dad, John, Bern, Loretta, and me in his car. People were sitting on top of people for the 450-mile trip to Niagara Falls. We went on all the activities available. We finished our sightseeing around 10 p.m. and headed toward our car. We went to the outdoor parking lot but couldn't find the car. Then we realized that we may have been in the wrong parking lot. No one knew where we had parked. We waited until 3 a.m., until all the cars in all the lots had left so we could locate our car. Always remember where you park.

Elementary School

I spent my first year in public school at P.S. 97, until my parents transferred me to St. Mary Mother of Jesus elementary school, which was around the block from my house. Actual nuns taught us. I remember only my sixth-, seventh-, and eighth-grade teachers, since they were special. I had a crush on my sixth-grade teacher, Sister Rosario. She was very sociable and played football with us in the street. Not the typical nun. I spent hours assembling and painting a plastic battleship and gave it to her as a present — why, I don't know. My seventh-grade teacher was Sister Janice. If you did something she didn't like, you had to hold out your hand while she hit it with the wooden pointer.

Sister Jean Helen, the eighth-grade teacher, had a thing with hair. If a girl teased her hair or a boy did not part his hair, the reward would be to have your hair washed in the sink by the teacher. If you were chewing gum in class, you would have to take it out of your mouth and put it in your hair. One of my classmates did not do his homework. This enraged Sister Jean Helen. She picked up the child's desk — with him in it — and threw it across the room. We had to learn — there was no choice. It was learn or die.

I read only comic books. I thought, *Why would anyone read a book that had no pictures?* The first book I read without pictures was in the eighth grade — *The Legend of Sleepy Hollow*, which I borrowed from a girl I liked. I was a little late to reading. Later in life, I became a voracious reader. As my reading volume and diversity improved, my handwriting "deproved." For example, one time Savia was ordering a book for me online, the title of which I had written down, but she couldn't read the title properly. She asked, "Was the book you wanted *Discovering Algeria?*" "No, it was *Reversing Alzheimer's.*" That is how illegible my handwriting had become. However, I did read everything, so a book titled *Discovering Algeria* was not entirely out of the question.

Since school was just around the block, Tommy and I walked to school together every day. I would stop at his house on the way. There was a TV show called "The Restless Gun." We would race home at lunch time and put on our holster and gun, so that at 12 noon, we could see if we could beat John Payne to the draw.

We would play Cowboys and Indians and once in a while go to the movies. We once saw the movie *Tarzan,* and it rubbed off so well, when we got home, we were swinging on tree branches like monkeys.

I liked this girl Cathy on our block but was not bold enough to ask her out. Instead, I asked all the kids in the neighborhood that we played with if they wanted to go roller skating in the arena a few blocks away. They all thought it was a great idea, however, their parents did not. The only one who could go was a not-so-attractive, weight-challenged girl in the neighborhood. I had a decision to make: Do I cancel and make her feel bad or go with her, looking like the bat-and-ball couple, or perhaps giving her the wrong impression. I decided to go. We skated together as partners, holding hands, and had a great time. I think I made the right decision.

Aunt Jo's sister-in-law, Suzie, would take the kids to the beach at Coney Island. My sister Loretta and cousins Johnny and Bernie could all swim. With Suzie's help, I later learned to swim at age 13. However, there was one problem with my swimming style. If I held a floating device in front of me and kicked my legs, I would go *backwards.* Somehow, I had the wrong leg or foot motion. I have since taken swimming lessons from many instructors, with no change. So, when I swim, I don't kick my feet because that would slow me down; I just use my arms and drag my legs behind me. Strange but true.

I never really thought of myself as mischievous, but now that I think back, that statement may need to be revisited. During Halloween, we would run a string from one side of the street to the other. In the middle of the string, we tied an effigy of a witch. When we saw a car coming down the block, we waited until it was near the string and then raised it to the level of the car's windshield to try to scare the driver. We could have caused a real accident. *What were we thinking?*

People who lived on the ground floor at Halloween might expect a ghost mask outside their window at night. However, if they lived on the second floor, that was definitely unexpected. So, we would put the mask on a tall pole to reach the second floor. I could tell by the screams that it did have the desired effect.

Music was a big deal for every generation. Rock 'n' Roll was just starting, and I was hooked. I would save my coins, and, when I had enough money, I would go to the record store on Bay Parkway to buy a 45-rpm (revolutions per minute) record to add to my record box collection. These records were made of vinyl and had grooves in them. The records would play on a turntable that spun at three different speeds, depending on the size of the record. There was a 7-inch record at 45 rpm for single songs, a 10-inch record at 78 rpm for the older songs, and a 12-inch record at 33⅓ rpm for albums. An arm with a needle would extend onto the record to produce the sound. I heard they're making a comeback.

In October 1957, Russia launched the first artificial Earth satellite. It was 23 inches around, the size of a beach ball, and made of polished metal. It was in a low orbit that circled the Earth every 96 minutes. I remember standing outside my parent's house, able to see the sun reflect on its shiny surface and thinking how amazing that was. It was also visible at night from the reflection of the moon. We would spot it as it slowly crossed the sky and then wait to see if we could catch its return.

In 1960, John F. Kennedy was campaigning for President. One of the campaign stops he made was on Bay Parkway and 86th Street in Brooklyn, a few blocks from my parent's house, so I went to see him. He was standing in the back of an open-bed car, greeting people. I was about one foot away from him. That was the closest I ever came to a President or future President.

High School 1960 to 1964

I was close to graduating elementary school, grades one through eight, and it was time to choose a high school. You could put five schools on your application to see which ones would accept you. I only had four chosen, so as a joke, I entered Xaverian High School. This was a very prestigious, all-male Catholic high school, for which I thought my chance of acceptance was zero. To my amazement, I was accepted. The freshmen were divided into 11 classes, 1A to 1K, based upon your score on the entrance exams. I was placed in 1J, which meant I was near the bottom of the intelligence range at the school. My progression went from 1J to 2H, then to 3F, and finally 4E. Learning became fun. The Xaverian brothers made you learn. You had no choice. They used teaching techniques not allowed today such as chalk- and book-throwing, ear-twisting, and the old standard, detention. Somehow, I loved learning there, especially math. My English teacher loved *The Canterbury Tales,* and, as a result, the class had to learn the first 14 lines of the Prologue in Old English. After almost 60 years, I can still recite this. That was the code you could use to determine if someone was in your class. My classmate Jim Basso also has this indelibly imprinted in his head.

When my daughters, Daria and Tara, were learning prepositions in school, I taught them the song I had learned in high school. So when they had a test to see how many prepositions they could name in 10 minutes, they listed all of the following: (sung to The Marine Hymn) "about, across, against, among, at, behind, beneath, between, during, for, in, near, off, over, through, to, under, up, with, above, after, along, around, before, below, upon, beyond, by, down, without, within, from, into, of, on, past, toward, until." It's amazing what you can memorize when it's put to music.

My parents were eager for me to learn to drive a car, so they would not have to bother Uncle Ralph for everything. By taking a Driver's Education course, you could get your driver's license at age 16 instead of the usual age of 17. I passed the driving test on the first try. Suzie played another role in my life besides swimming. My parents bought me my first car from Suzie for $125. It was a red and white 1956 Ford Fairlane.

I was now the designated family chauffeur. During the 1960s, cars had not yet been perfected. If you were taking a trip of 50 miles or more, you had to first check your motor oil, transmission fluid, and tires so you would have a reasonable chance of reaching your destination. It may be hard to imagine today, but there were always cars broken down on the side of the road. It is comparable to current computers,

Becoming Me (My Birth, Childhood, and School Years)

which are not quite yet perfected. My father worked at the bus depot about half mile from home. My car was not what you would call "fuel efficient". You could see the black smoke spewing from the car exhaust as you drove down the street. It could not be fixed. My father and I came up with a solution. He put motor oil and transmission fluid he got from work in glass gallons. We ran a siphon from the glass gallon to the engine, so we would have an endless supply of fluids and exhaust fumes. Even with these problems, it was still my first car and I loved it. I made an exact plastic replica of the car from a kit I purchased, and I painted it the same color as the real car. I put it near the back window. It looked unique and different until the summer heat came and melted it. Then it really looked different!

There was a girl I liked who lived across the street from me. Her name was Cathy Cozzi, the same girl I wanted to go roller skating with. Her parents were very strict with her. I asked her to a dance at my high school. Her father said she could go but only if he drove us to and from the dance. That was fine with me. The evening went well. I think Cathy did not accept her restrictive lifestyle, so she rebelled. She was hanging around the wrong type of people at night in the schoolyard at the public school a few blocks from her house. This went on for about a year until she felt so ashamed and inferior that she killed herself. The shades on the window across the street were closed in mourning for a very long time. The neighborhood was in shock. There is no handbook on parenting. You have to walk the line between too permissive and too strict.

60-Yard Dash

I was very thin in high school. As a matter of fact, I was thin for most of my life. Everyone else was on a diet trying to lose weight. I was always trying to gain weight. There were no organizations or clubs like Weight Watchers, etc., to help. Can't they watch the weight go up as well as go down? The second year, I joined the track team. We practiced at Fort Hamilton track. I was designated a sprinter and ran the 60-yard dash and 440-yard four-person relay. Practice was composed of a two-mile warm up run from the school to the Verrazano Bridge and back. Then the sprinters would perform their workout. Cool down would be the same two-mile run from the bridge and back. It seemed like a lot of effort and practice to run for six seconds in competition. Catholic high schools had different categories based upon weight. Midget class was less than 112 pounds. I qualified. Each year, I struggled but successfully made the weight class. By the third year of school, I had more experience, practiced more, and ran faster. This was a wonderful time for me since I was now competing against freshmen. They were the only ones who were in the same weight class as me! The same was true when I was a senior. By that time, I had the New York City outdoor record for the 60-yard dash. An important meet came up at Madison Square Garden. My school was competing with another school for first place, and I was to represent the school in the 60-yard dash. There were six lanes. I was in lane number six, and my fiercest competitor was in lane number one. The starting pistol fired, and we took off. I was running as fast as I could, all the time looking over to see where I was in relation to my competitor in lane one. I knew my team was counting on me to win this race. I used all the talents God gave me, and, at the very end of the race, I passed the competitor I was so worried about. A strange thing happened when the race was completed. I noticed that I was in the lane next to my competitor. This meant that I crossed lanes two, three, four, and five while I was running. I was disqualified for running out of my lane.

There is a moral to this story: Keep your eye on the goal, and don't be distracted by outside influences.

This story was posted on the bulletin board at Lakeland Air Force Base in Georgia by Robert (Beej) DuMont, a friend of the family and an Airman himself, to remind the soldiers to focus on their mission.

440-Yard Relay

It was a clear, crisp 63° day in 1963, when my 440-yard-relay team was to compete at the outdoor track at Iona College. The track at Iona College was a little different from other tracks we had competed on. It had "banked" turns. That meant when you ran on the turn, you would not be perpendicular to the ground but probably at a 45° angle. Each of four runners would run 110 yards — ¼ of a mile — and then pass a baton to the next runner. There was a designated range in which the baton had to be passed. If the baton was passed outside this range, your team was disqualified. The second, third, and fourth runners would mark the spot on the track with a piece of chalk — a stone or stick could also be used — to indicate when they are to start running. It was a "blind pass," meaning the receiving runner would start running and then put their left hand down in a cupped shape without looking until, hopefully, the baton hit. After many hours of trial and error during practice at school, each runner knew exactly how many steps it would take based upon the approaching runner's speed and your speed to effortlessly pass the baton without losing a step. At least, that is the theory. Scafidi, Denesopolis, and I marked our "take-off" spots. Vin Sulfaro would run the first leg of our team, and we expected him to be in the lead when he passed the baton. Our leadoff man the previous year, Charlie Spero, had been injured during an outdoor meet when the baton fell during the transfer and the runner from another team, who was wearing spikes, accidentally stepped on Charlie's hand, which required stitches. Who knew track could be so dangerous?

Vin placed his feet in the starting blocks until he heard the words "On your mark, set" and then the sound of the starter's gun. He took off and immediately led the pack of runners. When he handed the baton to me, the second leg, we were in first place. As I hit Scafidi's take-off spot, he took off and received the baton with an even bigger lead. When Scafidi hit Denesopolis' take-off spot, we had a comfortable lead. Denesopolis, the last leg, took the baton and did not let up. When he crossed the finish line, our team had covered the 440 yards in 47.8 seconds. Considering that, over the years, thousands of teams had run this exact distance before us, we were awed that we now "owned" the fastest time ever recorded in New York City track history.

The Potato Race

Each year, the school had a class tournament. One of the events was called "The Potato Race," held on the indoor basketball court. Each player would start on one side of the court, run 25 feet, pick up a small bowling pin, and run back to place it on the starting line. Then the player would pick up the next pin, placed 50 feet away, and bring that back to the starting line, then 75 feet, then 100 feet. Once all four pins had been placed on the starting line, you had to run back to the middle of the court — the finish line. The first person to cross the finish line won. I knew who the fast people in the school were. They were all on the track team. This event had no weight classes. My midget class did not matter. I was now competing with all the students. There were trials, quarter-finals, and semi-finals. The final came down to two competitors, me and Victor Galati, a track star who ran at the higher weight class. I wondered if I, the little midget, could beat him.

We both picked up the first pin and brought it back to the start; same for the second pin, and same for the third pin. During the entire race, you could not tell who was winning — it was that close. We both put our last pin on the line and ran toward the mid-court finish. I ran as fast as I could, knowing that I had a chance to win this. My body was running faster than my feet could carry me, so I fell head first across the finish line. So did Victor Galati. The judges said I won and awarded me the First Place trophy. This meant I was the best in the school at this event. After that, I was called "The Mighty Midget."

On November 22, 1963, I was sitting in the bleacher seats at my high school, watching a basketball game, when we heard the news over the loudspeaker. President Kennedy had been shot and killed. We didn't think that could happen in America, but it did. We were all stunned, and many were crying. It seems everyone knows where they were when they heard "The News."

During the last year of high school, I thought I wanted to become a policeman, since I liked helping people. I heard that the policeman's exam was being given at the 168 St. Armory. Fortunately, I knew exactly where it was, because I'd spent many Saturday afternoons running there in track meets. I would take the train from my house in Brooklyn, and it would take me about 2½ hours to get to the armory in the Bronx.

Becoming Me (My Birth, Childhood, and School Years)

The day of the test, I got up early, so I would arrive before the 10:00 a.m. exam. I reached the armory at 9:30 a.m. — in plenty of time before the start of the test. However, I couldn't find anyone. The place was empty. Eventually I did find someone who informed me that the policeman's exam was at the armory — but not the one in the Bronx. It was at the one in Queens. It was too late for the ride to Queens. I think I was being guided. I did want to help people, but being a policeman was not the route for me.

The St. Mary's track team, at my elementary school, for kids 10 to 16, needed an assistant coach, so I volunteered. The coach and I better categorized the runners into their appropriate events — sprinters, middle-distance, and long-distance runners. I then started timing the kids during practice and at their track meets. I kept track of personal-best times and team records for each event. It turned out that this had not been done before. The results were both motivational and astounding. Many of our runners were now at the top of their class, and our team won many track meets. I was assistant coach from 1965 to 1968. This helped nurture my love of statistics.

College 1964 to 1968

In 1964, I started college at St. John's University in downtown Brooklyn. It would take me about an hour by train to get to school. I was having difficulty and failed many tests in chemistry with Mrs. Correo, an Army Sergeant type of teacher. My parents hired a tutor for me, Robert Rome, who came to our home. He made chemistry interesting. He showed me that heating or cooling chemicals could change their color, since the temperature change made new chemicals. Different chemicals made crystals of different shapes and sizes. It may sound dull, but the idea of understanding nature was fascinating to me. After some tutoring, I decided to major in chemistry. A good teacher makes all the difference. When I speak to someone who dislikes math, I tell them it's not that you can't understand math, it's that you had a poor teacher.

If you ask any chemistry major, they will probably tell you that Organic Chemistry is the worst course they had to endure. The standard chemistry book is filled with formulas and reactions to memorize. It appears daunting. My Organic Chemistry teacher was Maureen O'Sullivan. She looked like a double of Maureen O'Hara from the 1952 movie *The Quiet Man*. A real beauty. Her style of teaching was reasoning. We did not use a book. She taught us how to use reason to determine how combining chemicals would react. It was my favorite class. I couldn't wait to take a test to impress her with how much I knew.

The last two years at St. John's were at the Jamaica Campus, a 2½-hour trip by train one way. It was the last year of chemistry, and, on the opposite end of the spectrum was our Analytical Chemistry teacher, Harry Horan. He had been teaching Analytical Chemistry for 35 years and had tenure; you could tell he didn't care. He would sit at his desk in the front of the class and read the text to us in a low, inaudible voice. It didn't matter what went on in the classroom; his eyes never strayed from the book. We learned nothing. There was one test where I failed but scored the highest mark in the class, 59 — and I was proud of it!

Becoming Me (My Birth, Childhood, and School Years)

When the course was finished, we thought we would pay a tribute to our infamous teacher. The class prepared a life-sized stuffed dummy representing Harry, and everyone met on the Sunken Meadow State Park beach on Long Island, where we would be less conspicuous. The first step was to prepare a fire on the beach and roast the dummy. We stood around the fire telling Harry stories. Next, we took the remains of the dummy, placed them in a bottle, and threw it into the ocean. A good time was had by all — except, of course, Harry. Yes, I guess that was mean, but we meant no harm, and it added to our fond and lasting memories of him.

The custom at the time was to take a road trip to Florida after graduation. I went with three of my classmates, Richard Martorano, Frank Leone, and Dennis Filangeri. Frank borrowed his father's Buick Riviera for the trip. It was a brand-new, elegant, top-of-the-line luxury vehicle. With four drivers, we took turns driving non-stop to Miami. Some of the roads on the way down had no speed limits. It was my turn to drive while everyone else was sleeping in the car. I was on a two-lane highway, one in each direction, and I was driving at 85 mph. The car in front of me was probably going 70, so I decided to pass it. I moved over to the other lane to pass and immediately saw a car approaching off in the distance.

So, I have a math question for you. If you are going 85 mph, and the approaching car is going 85 mph, how much time would you have to pass the car that was going 70 mph? The answer is "Almost none." So, when I moved into the left lane, I had to speed up to 100 and quickly swerve back into my lane, cutting off the 70 mph car just in time to avoid the oncoming car. The swerve woke all the sleeping passengers, who wondered what was going on. I told them that everything

Becoming Me (My Birth, Childhood, and School Years)

was alright — I just had to make a fast turn. The entire non-stop trip from New York to Florida took 24 hours.

We visited the Aquarium and the beaches and had a wonderful time.

We met three girls who were also on vacation. No appropriate stories here because then I would have to change the names to protect the innocent! On the drive back, we noticed that the car would not turn off. So, even when we stopped for gas, we had to leave the engine running. We did make it back home surprisingly, however, the engine wires and spark plugs were fried, and Frank's father's new car had to be junked.

National Guard 1969 to 1975

When I graduated college in 1968, the Vietnam War was in full swing. In 1965, President Johnson sent an additional 20,000 troops to Vietnam. All males between ages 18 and 25 were required to register for the draft. Each of the 365 days of the year was drawn randomly from a lottery to determine the order of drafting.

The National Guard was supposed to protect U.S. citizens within the U.S., although there was a small possibility that they would also be called upon to serve overseas. My options were to wait and see if my draft number was called, and then I would most certainly end up in Vietnam, or see if I could join the National Guard, where my chances to avoid the war were better.

I decided that the National Guard was a better bet. However, there was a waiting list to join the Guard. My draft number might be called before I had a chance to join. I was in luck. My roommate, Bob Lund, was a Sergeant in the Morristown, New Jersey, National Guard and would help me join. When I told my cousin Vinny Bertino about the options, he was also eager to join with me. Service in the National Guard consisted of eight weeks' Basic Training and eight weeks of advanced training in your specialized field, just like the regular Army. In addition to that, for the next

Becoming Me (My Birth, Childhood, and School Years)

six years, you had to serve one weekend every month and two weeks each summer.

The night before I left for Basic Training, I was at Savia's parents house in Queens. She gave me a St. Christopher medal to wear to keep me safe. I left her house and was driving home. As I was driving, I heard a metal-on-metal sound and saw the sky light up. I was not sure what that sound was. I looked up and saw a large tractor trailer on the curved overpass above me screeching against the guard rail. Then it fell off the overpass onto the road below, crushing the car behind me. Good thing I had that St. Christopher medal! I drove home at about 10 miles per hour with my legs shaking.

The next day, August 5, 1969, I left by train for four months, eight weeks of which was Basic Training in Ft. Campbell, Kentucky. Although I had been on vacation out of state with my parents and lived one hour away in New Jersey, it felt like this was the first time I was actually away from home — an eerie, almost-out-of-body experience.

It was interesting to meet people from all over the country. I got to be good friends with Richard Foster, from Ohio, and John Elder, a descendant of "The Sons of Katie Elder," among others. Look it up.

We all were indoctrinated with army haircuts. The Army barber would ask, "Do you want a crew cut, Mohawk, or flat top?" The end result was that we all had our heads shaved clean — regardless of our choice. We also received vaccination shots. The soldiers would walk shirtless in single file past two medics, one on each side. Each medic held a vaccination gun with about five needles. The goal was to have both guns work simultaneously. The medic on one side would shoot your upper arm, and you had to not flinch, or the needles would rip through your other arm. That in itself was a lesson in discipline.

We started the day at 4:00 a.m., when the lights went on in the barracks. Your feet were expected to hit the floor simultaneously when the lights went on. First, exercises, and then a mile run before breakfast. The assortment of food was amazing — waffles, pancakes, eggs any style, cereal, bagels, muffins, oatmeal, and all types of fruit. The problem was you had seven minutes to eat before the next group of soldiers arrived to take your seat. After about two weeks, the men started complaining. "The same old breakfast. Don't you have anything else to eat?"

There were various exercises, skills, and tests we had to pass to complete Basic Training. There was the firemen's carry. We were paired with soldiers of approximately the same weight. I was 125 pounds, as was the person I was to carry. I ran 100 yards there and 100 yards back, carrying him on my shoulder, fireman style, and then he carried me. It definitely was a way to build up your muscles and stamina. By the end of Basic, we still had the same partners. However, I now weighed 145 pounds, and my partner was 185 pounds. It sure was challenging.

As part of our training, we crawled through barbed wire in the mud with machine guns firing just over our heads. We were also trained in hand-to-hand combat, bayonets, grenades, and the M-16 rifle.

I was very nervous the day of grenade training. I had this premonition of getting nervous after pulling the pin on the grenade and dropping it in front of me. Fortunately, this did not happen, and I survived.

Becoming Me (My Birth, Childhood, and School Years)

When you fire the M-16 rifle, you have to put your cheek next to the rifle to align the sights in the middle and end of the barrel. My cheek was a little too close to the rifle when I was firing it, which made my teeth bleed. Then I learned the correct way to hold the rifle and later received a "Sharpshooter" medal for accuracy. After getting up early, exercising, training, and running, I was exhausted. Whenever we were in class, I had to fight to stay awake. I am sure I missed some important information, but I didn't care. The last week of Basic, everyone received their new orders, which detailed their advanced training and where it would be.

Since I had a Bachelor's degree in chemistry, the Army decided that I should be a Cannoneer, a person who loads howitzers. So, for my Advanced Training, I was on my way to Fort Sill, Oklahoma, to learn about howitzers. A howitzer is like a stationary tank that stays back about 20 miles from the actual battlefront and fires shells at the enemy position. My job was to load the howitzer with its 95-pound shells. Since I weighed 145 pounds, it was very difficult to lift the shells about four feet into the breech, or chamber. At the beginning of our training, two empty 55-gallon drums were placed at the back of the howitzer. I was on the side of the howitzer with earplugs. When the howitzer was fired, the sound waves knocked over both drums as a warning that you don't want to stand there.

I was always a little finicky about my food. Carrots could not touch the potatoes; meat cannot touch the string beans. You get the picture. I was in for a lesson in Army food etiquette. We were out in the field training in the rain when it was time for lunch. Each of us waited in the "chow line" until

it was our turn. At the first food station, salad was put on my plate; at the second food station, meat was added (on top of the salad), then mashed potatoes, then carrots, and finally ice cream as the dessert. This mixed well with the rain. My finicky food traits no longer seemed to be a problem. I did try coffee for the first time and didn't like it. The only time I drink coffee now is when I feel a headache starting. This is about once every two years since age 58. Before that, there were no headaches or coffee.

After weeks of lifting 95-pound rounds, wearing heavy helmets all day and running with substantial backpacks, my back gave out. The last couple of weeks, I was in and out of the infirmary and had difficulty bending to make my bed. Advanced Training was over, and I was sent home. This did not improve my back. I was sent to Army doctors, who took

Becoming Me (My Birth, Childhood, and School Years)

X-rays while I was standing, moving, and lifting weights. They did see a problem. Savia and I went to a well-known, highly regarded orthopedic surgeon in Morristown, who also took X-rays. He said, "You have deteriorated disks in your spine. Don't do any heavy lifting. Don't lift anything from the trunk of your car. Even if you avoid these activities, in a few years, you will not be able to walk." As you can imagine, I was kind of depressed walking to my car. Savia looked at me and said, "What does he know? That's his opinion. He is not a god. Let's see what we can do." I had to love her spunk, optimism, and inspiration.

Savia and I went to an introductory lecture by Dr. Sottille, a chiropractor in Parsippany. We made an appointment to be examined. He said my vertebrae were misaligned and needed to be adjusted. However, he thought Savia was in worse shape than me. We both went for adjustments about three times each week for a while, and now, 40 years later, our backs are still going strong. I am sure there is a lesson here. Can you guess what it is?

Basic and Advanced Training were behind me. Now it was one weekend each month and two weeks during the summer for six years as part of the National Guard. There was not much to do during our weekend training. I remember being given the task of cleaning the coffee pot. That was a real treat. I spent the entire day meticulously cleaning the coffee pot. It was something to do.

Becoming Me (My Birth, Childhood, and School Years)

Most of the time, the two-week training took place at Camp Drum in upstate New York. We usually made the six-hour trip in the back of a 2½-ton Army truck with bench seats along both sides. I was surprised to see that shortly after we left the armory in Morristown, the festivities would begin. A bottle of alcohol would be passed clockwise from one soldier to another, while a cigarette of marijuana would be passed counterclockwise. This seemed to be the accepted routine for the trip to camp. I took my place in passing the goods but did not partake. *These were our soldiers?*

Another summer, I was asked if I wanted to drive the Sergeant up to Camp Drum. I jumped at the opportunity to avoid the party I knew would take place in the back of the truck again that year. The jeep was already running when I climbed into the driver's seat, with the Sergeant as the passenger, waiting in line to begin the caravan to Camp Drum. It was then that I realized the jeep was a stick shift. I only knew how to drive an automatic-shifting car. I asked the Sergeant if he knew how to drive a stick shift, thinking he could guide me through the process. He did not know, either. There was a diagram on the handle of the shift indicating where first, second, third, and fourth gears were. I was able to have the jeep move in first gear, all the while repeating to myself, "First, first, first, first." This was the only way I could remember which gear I was in before attempting to switch to the next gear. As the speed increased, I shifted to second gear while repeating to myself, "Second, second, second, second." This was working fine until the caravan stopped in the center of Morristown, and my jeep stalled. All the vehicles in front of me started to move, leaving me behind at a busy intersection. I did not know how to restart the jeep. I frantically looked for keys, buttons, or switches to restart the jeep. The soldier in the jeep behind came up to me and showed me a button on the floor of the jeep that I needed to step on to start the jeep. The journey continued. We continued on the six-hour trek to Camp Drum. With me silently repeating "Second, second, third, third" all the way. After two weeks of driving every day, I was a stick-shift pro — no silent reminders necessary. That is how I learned to drive a stick shift.

I became friends with Peter Loeb, a person in our unit. He had a PhD in economics. We would hang out together at our two-week summer camp. He presented himself as "The Doctor." If anyone had a minor injury or a psychological problem, they would go to "The Doctor" for treatment. We all knew he was not a medical doctor, but nobody cared.

One evening, our barracks had a party and invited some girls from the town. Yes — those type of girls. Soldiers from the other barracks came to crash the party and were turned away. When the party was over, we fully expected the turned-away soldiers to attack us with full force. Peter and I were very nervous about the prospect of the other soldiers attacking us at night while we were asleep. We finagled a small room to sleep in. We locked our door, wrapped chains around the door handle, and attached the other side of the chain to the bed. We slept with the only weapon we had by our side, a shovel. Fortunately, we were not attacked at night. However, the next morning, the soldiers from our own unit pulled the pins in the hinges and easily removed the door. So much for our brilliant security plan!

As it turned out, my draft number never came up, therefore, I would not have been called to active service.

After experiencing just a minor taste of military life, I want to thank all our military for their service. We truly live in the home of the free because of the brave.

Hair Challenged

My dentist, Dr. D'Agostino, wore a hairpiece. He noticed that my hair was on its way out and mentioned an alternative. He said that there was a dermatologist, Dr. Norman Orentreich, in Manhattan, who'd pioneered this new procedure that could give you hair. I went for a consultation. What they do is actually transplant the hair from the back of your head to the top. They said the procedure would take about two hours, and you could be back to work the next day. I agreed to have the procedure done. The thought of hair again was something I was looking forward to. I am going to get a little gory here, so skip the next paragraph if you are squeamish.

They put needles with an anesthetic in the back of my head, the donor site, and the front of my head, the recipient site, to deaden the pain. The needles themselves were excruciating. Then, after that took effect, they would take a hole-punch type of instrument and remove small circles of scalp on the top of your head. Then, with the same instrument, they would remove circles of scalp containing 10 to 15 hair follicles and relocate/transplant it to the front, orienting the hair follicles in the correct direction. Because of the anesthetic, there was no pain, but the sounds of the doctor making holes in your head was not pleasant. Before you left, they would give you medication to take during recovery and wrap your head in a gauze turban. And they said I could go back to work the next day. I guess that was *technically* possible, but I felt a little uncomfortable with the turban and blood dripping down my face, so I stayed home for a while. This was the first session of many. I did buy a full-head wig until the scabs from the transplant healed and I was ready for a smaller hairpiece until the hair grew.

I did not go for as many sessions as was necessary for a fuller look, but I had had enough. I did wear a hairpiece for a while — even at my wedding — and it looked good. Whenever it rained, I had to use an umbrella. When it was windy, I had to wear a hat.

One Sunday, on the way home from visiting my parents, I got into the car and removed my annoying hairpiece so I could "be free." We arrived home late at night. The next morning was windy and rainy. I was getting dressed to go to work but couldn't find my hairpiece. I looked everywhere and couldn't locate it. I looked outside my upstairs bedroom window and saw it being blown from one end of the yard to the other. It must have fallen off my lap when I got out of the car.

That was the end. My father, who was also bald, had a sign in his front foyer that read "God made just so many perfect heads — the rest he had to cover with hair." Now, I rarely use hats or umbrellas. It's only water.

Years later, a relative went to have a minor hair procedure performed, so I went to support her and show her that I was having the procedure done also. When I told the doctors that I'd previously had a hair transplant performed by Dr. Orentreich, they called in all the doctors in the office to marvel at his work, knowing that he was the person who'd pioneered the procedure.

Me as Me (My Career)

Warner Lambert

I graduated from St. John's in May 1968 with a Bachelor's degree in Chemistry and was anxious to join the workforce. I sent out resumes everywhere and went on several job interviews. I traveled on a small plane for an interview at Ayers Labs, a pharmaceutical company in Rousses Point, New York, a stone's throw from the Canadian border. It seemed like I was in the middle of nowhere. In my mind, I did have limits on what I would do for a job. By August, my limits were gone, and I would go anywhere.

I heard about the Shamrock Employment Agency, in Connecticut, which had been successful in placing scientists like me. I drove to Connecticut to meet with the agency personnel. My mother came along for the ride. She loved car rides and experiencing new scenery. It seems there was an opening in a pharmaceutical company in Morris Plains, New Jersey, that was looking for a chemist. It was hard to believe that from Brooklyn, I had to go to Connecticut to find a job in New Jersey.

I met with the head of Quality Control, who asked me many questions about my background. During the interview, I told him I'd attended school at St. John's in Jamaica. He asked what it was like attending school in another country. I said "Jamaica, Queens, New York." Again, Mom came along for the ride and was in my car in the parking lot just outside his window.

The interview went well, and I started work on Monday, August 12, 1968 as a lab technician. My job was to chemically test the ingredients and the finished products the company produced for content and quality. Brian La Bar was the supervisor, while some of the lab technicians were Jon L. Hauge ("L" stood for "Lance"), Joe Notary, Jay Zwiekel, and Frank Castro. It was an unusual group. None of them had been born in New Jersey. I thought everyone in New Jersey was imported. As a matter of fact, I met my first native New Jersian after three years.

Work ended at 4:24 p.m. every day. **Jay Zwiekel** and I both headed to Brooklyn on Friday after work to see our families. At 4:23 p.m., we would use the lab door saddle as the starting block for the race home. We would get down on our hands in a starting position. When the bell rang at 4:24, we dashed down the hall into our cars and used different routes to get to the toll booth at the Verrazano Bridge. We would note the time and compare it on Monday morning to see who had won the race for that week.

Joe Notary was a philosopher, math genius, strongman, and eating champion. At one of the usual weekend gatherings, he picked me up and put me in a tree in front of his house.

There was an all-you-can-eat chicken restaurant that looked like a barn silo on the intersection of Route 10 and Route 202 that was called "Drummers Corner." All of us went to the restaurant. We first ordered a pizza, and then we ate all the chicken they had until the restaurant had to close. We did have some champion eaters in the group, especially Joe. He was a real character.

Joe had a big test coming up in school that he was not prepared for. He pulled the fire alarm, which evacuated the building, giving him more study time.

In another exciting chapter in the lab, Joe was reading instructions to test an ingredient. The instructions read "Heat either ethanol or propanol in a flask...." He read this as "*ether*, ethanol, or propanol...." He placed ether in the flask and placed the flame under it. Ether is flammable and combustible. Again, the lab was evacuated; however, this time it was unintentional.

Frank Castro lived close to work and traveled by bicycle instead of by car. We were paid on Fridays. One Friday when I did not have to race to Brooklyn, I went to the bank to cash my check. Only the drive-up window was open. There was a line of cars waiting their turn, and guess who was in the middle of the line among the cars with his bike? Frank. The scene was hysterical.

Brian La Bar was our lab supervisor when I first started. Brian and Jon shared an apartment until Brian was called to active duty in the Army.

Joanne Martin spent her summer internship in our lab. She'd gone to school in Omaha, Nebraska, to become a pediatrician. We wrote back and forth a few times and then I lost track of her. In 1978, I was hospitalized for chest pains at Morristown Memorial Hospital and found out that Joanne had become a heart surgeon. I asked if she could visit me. She did, and we reminisced about our days in the lab together. The same thing happened in 1990, when, again, I had undiagnosed chest pains. She came to visit.

Jon Hauge and I became good friends. Jon was a fantastic singer — me, not so much. We would have our cue words that began our songs in the lab. For example, Jon would say, "Bob, what are you doing tonight?" I would say "Tonight," and we would then both start singing the song "Tonight" from *West Side Story*.

Jon got me interested in the Masterwork Choir in Morristown. We practiced the "Carmina Burana" in Latin for weeks before our first performance at the Garden State Arts Center, now the Prudential Center in Holmdel, New Jersey. Standing in the middle of all those angelic voices made it sound like you were really in heaven. We would be accompanying the New Jersey Symphony Orchestra. This was a big deal. I invited everyone I knew, including my parents, who traveled from Brooklyn to attend. The rehearsal started, and the conductor noticed that I was reading the words in the pamphlet we were using. He immediately removed me from the choir because he said it would be dark during the performance and that, if I didn't know the words, I would not be in the performance. What a shock! If he had mentioned during our rehearsals that all lines needed to be memorized, that's what I would have done. Instead I was in the audience with my family, who had traveled from New York to see me perform with the New Jersey Symphony Orchestra. I later found out that this conductor was notorious for not letting the singers know what was expected and then removing them for not being prepared. I left the choir.

One day after work around 5 p.m., I got a call from Jon. He said he was hungry and asked if I wanted to go out to

Me as Me (My Career)

dinner with him. I told him I was going to see my college friend Ronnie Sica (now Valente) in New Brunswick and invited him to accompany me. We could eat there. We arrived at about 6:30 and found Ronnie at the library preparing for a test. We spoke for a while and found out she had already eaten. Going to dinner would be awkward, so we didn't. We started back, thinking we could eat at the Morristown Diner when we arrived home. Jon and I were having a great discussion about the evening we'd had and issues at work. As we were driving home, we noticed that the road was unfamiliar. We kept driving for a while until we were able to get off at an exit and find a gas station, where we could ask for directions. I got out of the car and asked the gas-station attendant how far it was to Morristown. He stopped for a moment and walked over to the other attendant and asked, "Hey, Jim. Have you ever heard of Morristown?" Then we knew we were really lost. It seems that, as we were talking, we'd accidentally taken the ramp for 78 West and ended up deep into Pennsylvania. We did have pizza for dinner at Cutters in Morristown at 3 a.m. Jon was *really hungry* by then.

Savia and I introduced Jon to one of Savia's friends. This was our first encounter with matchmaking. Over the years, we accumulated an exemplary record. We introduced four people to friends we knew, and, in six months, they were married. The unusual part was that they did not marry the people we introduced them to. But so what? Mission accomplished.

Living Arrangements

For the first three months at Warner Lambert, I commuted from my home in Brooklyn to Morris Plains, New Jersey, about an hour and 10 minute drive. After a while, it seemed more reasonable to get a place closer to work. I rented a room at the YMCA in Morristown, now Courthouse Plaza, for $72 a month. It sounds like a low price because you get what you pay for. My room could fit my bed and the space to walk around three sides of the bed. It had a corner window, but there was a large beehive outside, so I did not dare open the window. There was a community bathroom down the hall. There was a swimming pool downstairs, and I signed up for swimming lessons. Although I learned to swim when I was 13, I knew I needed much improvement. After many swimming lessons, nothing had changed. I still swam backwards if I used my legs. But what did happen was that I met one of the other people in the class taking lessons. His name was L. Robert Lund, better known as Bob Lund. The L. stood for Llewellyn, but he kept that a secret. He did not like that name. After attending several lessons together, he asked if I wanted to share an apartment with him. I said I did not know him well enough and we had to get to know each other better first.

Instead, I rented a room at 54 Olyphant Drive in Morristown on the third floor. I'd inherited all my cooking skills from my father. He could probably boil water, but I am not sure since I had never seen it, so Mom would make food for me during the weekend to bring back on Monday. I went back to Brooklyn on Wednesday after work for food refills. Occasionally, I would make pasta using the sauce Mom gave me.

As I slept in bed at night, I could feel the bed swaying. I assumed it was because I was on the third floor of the house and there were heavy trucks passing by on the streets below. During the Christmas season, even though I was there by myself, I decorated a Christmas tree with balls, lights, and

Me as Me (My Career)

tinsel — the whole shebang. As I was lying in bed, I heard noises coming from the room with the tree. It made me wonder. Were the trucks really responsible for my swaying bed, or was it something else? I grabbed a flashlight, got out of bed, and faced the Christmas tree. Then I saw it. The cat from the owner downstairs had come into my room and was climbing the tree! Mystery solved.

After a year at Olyphant Drive, I took Bob Lund's offer, and we rented an apartment at the Quincy Arms at 60 Elm Street in Morristown. It had a kitchenette, living room, and bedroom, with two single beds on the ground floor. The driveway to the apartment complex was level with our bedroom windows. It would not be easy, but there was a possibility a

drunk driver could come right through our windows. Bob and I made this our home. We bought a fish tank and two fish. Bob named the fish "Robert" after himself and "Ralph," my middle name or so I thought. See page 164. Bob and I went food shopping together. I would always talk to the checkout people, so Bob gave me the title "Social Butterfly." He meant it as a compliment.

 I asked Bob if he was ever married, and he said, "I could marry anyone I please. I just don't please anyone." He was engaged once, but that is as close as he got to marriage. My wedding to Savia was getting closer, and I did not know how to dance, so I thought I would surprise her. Bob and I took dancing lessons at the Arthur Murray Studios with instructor Lynn Camissa. We had a ball laughing through the entire lesson and learning at the same time.

 When I returned from the Army, I went back to work at Warner Lambert. In 1973, I decided to also go back to school at Seton Hall in South Orange for an MBA in Finance. However, there were some remnants of Army life that interfered with my education. In the Army, I would get up early, run a mile or more, do strenuous exercises all day, and then attend a lecture on some military topic. But after the exhaustive day, I would sleep through the lecture. This programming did not stop after the Army. Whenever the teacher would stand in front of the class, I would immediately fall asleep. I thought I had a solution to my problem. There was a product at that time called "NoDoz" — it was straight caffeine. So, five minutes before the teacher would start class, I would go to the bathroom, wash my face with cold water, and take my NoDoz tablet, thinking that would help. No effect. As a result, I failed the class.

Me as Me (My Career)

The next year, I was ready to give it another try. I attended night school at Fairleigh Dickinson University in Florham Park. Savia and I came home for dinner, and then she accompanied me to school. She stayed in the library, studying Interior Decorating, while I attended my classes. My ability to concentrate had changed. When I would study for a test, I noticed that I could not focus too well. I timed how long I could focus before my mind started to wander. It was 10 seconds! I didn't realize concentration and focus are like a muscle and atrophies with lack of use. I worked on this muscle until it was back in shape. I attended classes for three years at night until I graduated in 1976 with a Master's Degree in Finance.

As a **Lab Analyst,** I spent about three years in the lab testing ingredients and finished products for identification

and potency. While testing products, we found it amusing to coat our arms with acetone to produce a white film. Later we found out it was a carcinogen. My favorite smell in the lab was aniline. It had a sweet almond aroma. Later, we found out it was *also* a poisonous carcinogen. We would make a paste of a compound called Potassium Permanganate and paint the lab floor with it. As someone would walk into the lab, there would be crackling and sparks under their shoes. Somehow it seemed funny at the time.

While working in the lab, I decided to organize a Decathlon at my house and invite many of the people from work. The 10 events included Running, Chess, Pool, Ping Pong, and Checkers, among others I can't remember. There was an elaborate scoring system for each event and finally the total point score. At the end, I gave out trophies and ribbons as prizes, and we all had a wonderful day. It seems that this event was noticed by upper management (because I'd invited them) and was responsible for my first job outside the lab. You may think that was a shrewd move to be noticed and get ahead. But honestly, I just did it for the fun. As **Quality Control Auditor,** I would audit the manufacturing processes and write a procedure documenting each step. During one of my audits, I noticed an inconsistency in how the different departments would assign an expiration date on the finished product. One department would assign the expiration date based upon when the tablets were compressed, another when the bottles containing the tablets were filled, and another when ingredients were combined. I met with the head of the Quality Control Department, my boss's boss. He had a doctorate in Chemistry and was a Rhodes Scholar — very impressive credentials. I explained my findings to him. *He said that if I*

Me as Me (My Career)

discussed this with anyone, he would have me fired. That was not the reaction I thought I would receive. I wrote my report and handed it to my boss. I am not sure what happened, but the procedure was changed so that all the expiration dates were assigned consistently, and I still had a job. About nine months later, the Rhodes Scholar didn't.

As Quality Control Auditor, I also audited outside companies who sent their products to Warner Lambert. I was auditing a company in Virginia, so I stayed overnight. Savia came with me. When the audit was over, the gentleman asked if I wanted to go to lunch. I said that my wife was in the hotel and asked how he felt about her joining us. That was OK with him. We were talking at lunch when he said that he worked part-time at a university helping people overcome their fears through hypnotism. Savia and I thought that was an interesting topic to discuss. During these sessions with clients, he said that he'd come across something unexpected. Some people spoke in a different language, a language they did not know, while they were hypnotized; others explained how they had drowned and were afraid of water. It seemed to him that many had previous lives. When one woman was hypnotized, she started crying and saying, "What are they doing to him?" Further inquiry uncovered that she was at the foot of the cross when Jesus was crucified.

He said he was not ready for this type of reaction when he started his practice but that, through his sessions with his clients, he now believed in past lives. He said that most souls were here before and that there were not many "new" souls being created. After all these years, I still remember this unusual experience.

After about two years, I went from Quality Control to **Supervisor of Chemical Weighing** in Manufacturing. This was the department that weighed all the raw materials and ingredients that were sent to manufacturing to be combined to make the finished products. I had a group of about 10 employees whom I supervised, including Art Flynn, the group leader. I would go home and tell Savia I didn't know what I was doing. How could I supervise employees when I didn't know the job? She gave me good advice: "Wait a month, and you will have learned the job." She was right. All the departments would send their requests to Chemical Weighing, so the ingredients would be measured and ready when production started. It seemed many of the departments could not schedule properly to give me enough lead time to weigh the batches. This resulted in constant emergency requests and was disrupting my department. I met with each of the offending department heads individually and helped them schedule, so they could interact better with my department. My department was now working efficiently. Every day, I would place a word problem on the corkboard where the employees gathered before work began. They enjoyed trying to solve the puzzle and discussing it.

There was one administrative issue that comes to mind. On the rare occasion that something was urgent, I would write "Expedite" on it and give it to my secretary, Susan. Weeks went by, and I received a call from someone looking for their raw materials. I asked Susan about it and discovered that she thought "Expedite" meant "Discard."

On another occasion, I was standing in the middle of the staging area where the chemicals are weighed, talking to some employees, when something poked me in the side. My first reaction was to force my elbow back with as much power as I had. When I turned around and looked back, I saw a girl curled up on the floor holding her stomach. "Sorry, Helen — it was an accident!"

When Quality Control was establishing a new department, they asked me to go in and set up all the procedures, systems, and workflows, since they knew I had helped them in the past. I was honored.

Art Flynn, the group leader, and I became good friends. We advertised in the newspapers for handyman work. Surprisingly, we got some jobs. We trimmed bushes, dug up plants, and did some outside painting. One woman we did painting for "liked" Art. She said her boat was in South Carolina and asked if we could help her sail it to New York. Being a little crazy at the time, we told her we would think about it. When we came to our senses, we turned down the job.

Art and his wife had four boys. One day when Art was watching them, one of the boys fell out of the tree he was climbing, hit his head, and died. Art's wife blamed him, and I think he blamed himself. He was not the same after that. He started drinking, staying out late at night; he saw other girls and fell into a depression. He attempted suicide a few times and spent some time in a mental hospital. I haven't heard from Art in many years, and I'm not sure what became of him.

After about two years, I left Chemical Weighing and got a job as **Supervisor of Granulating.** Even though I thought I made tremendous improvements while in Chemical Weighing, the next person who took over had a new outlook and made even further improvements. It is true that we stand on the shoulders of those who have come before us.

In this department, the ingredients are combined into cylinders, mixed until the ingredients are uniform, and then compressed into tablet form. The equipment here was complicated, and a fair amount of skill and a certain level of constant attention were needed to perform the task properly. I supervised about 15 employees. Two of them were borderline alcoholics. Before I would let them start work each day, they were required to come to my office, take my pen apart, and put it back together. If they passed this test, they were allowed to work. If not, I sent them home.

My next stop was **Supervisor of Coating.** This department required the most skill for the operator of the equipment. The raw, compressed tablet was loaded into a rotating cylinder while the operator would slowly pour ingredients into the cylinder. Some ingredients were liquid, like shellac secretions from insect larva, while others were powders. Coating was a combination of art and science. The operator had to know when to add the coating ingredients, how long it should dry, and when to add the next layer of coating material. Needless to say, this was difficult. I started collecting a Dixie cup full of any batch of material that looked a little "funny." Every Friday afternoon, I got all 25 operators and the group leader together to discuss the "funny" tablets I had collected. This improved the quality of our batches.

However, it seemed that the Quality Control Department was rejecting more and more of our production, while I was thinking that the quality was improving. After much thought and investigation, I suspected that the problem was the result of a new Head of Quality Control. I put together a graph of our monthly production over the past three years and the percentage rejection rate. The graph showed a slow but steady increase in approved batches followed by a peak and then a steady decline in approvals. The beginning of the decline coincided exactly with the start of a new Head of Quality

Me as Me (My Career)

Control. I circulated a memo disclosing my data and arguing that inspection criteria are not supposed to change depending on who is the head of the department. I made a good case that improved our batches being accepted.

There was a disciplinary system used at that time as follows: a minor infraction would result in what was called Step 1, the next incident would be Step 2, next was Step 3, and then you would be fired for any further problem. There was an incident in the Liquid Manufacturing Department in which an operator added the wrong ingredient to a batch and cost the company significant dollars. The operator was placed on Step 3, which meant that any further mistake, no matter how small, would get him fired. The operator was afraid to work.

While I was the head of Coating, one of my employees accidentally added Dusting Powder to the batch instead of Chalkless Dusting Powder. Both labels were white and could easily have been confused. My boss asked me to place the operator on Step 3, since a precedent had been set weeks earlier in the Liquid Manufacturing Dept. I explained to my boss that the accident was as much our fault — for not distinguishing the similar powders more clearly through better labeling — as it was the operator's. My boss disagreed and said that Step 3 was warranted since it was consistent with the previous incident. I told him that placing the operator in the other department on Step 3 was a mistake that I did not want to perpetuate and that I would not place the operator on Step 3. Since I would not, he placed him on Step 3 and told me I had six months to find another position. It seemed that my Catholic background had instilled in me to always do the right thing, regardless of the consequences. I am not sure if that is good, bad, idealistic, or naive.

Warner Lambert, fortunately, had an excellent internal job-posting system for all company job openings. The General Diagnostics division of Warner Lambert was looking for a **Quality Control Manager.** The people in that division were somehow aware that my sense of doing the right thing could not be compromised and thought Quality Control was a good fit.

I was now in charge of 10 inspectors and a group leader who examined all materials that came into the building or left the building. This included bottles, bottle caps, packaging materials, chemicals, tablets, and liquids. As I said, we inspected everything that came in and everything that went out. It seemed that, for all the years that this department had existed, there was no overall, comprehensive written manual describing what defects to look for and how important or serious each defect was. So Mike Donovan, the group leader, and I took on the challenge. How else could we properly perform our job? What did the people before us do?

I didn't know, and it didn't matter. We spent the first two hours of every workday uninterrupted, writing the "Quality Control Inspection Manual." Every material that entered or left the building needed to have an inspection protocol. We contacted each supplier and discussed the defects we had found, what defects they looked for, and the severity of the defect. We then formulated our criteria for review and arrived at our final inspection parameters. It took Mike and I a little more than two years to complete the manual. At first — and even second — it appeared that this task was too big for us. But meeting regularly every day and persistence made it possible. Most tasks, even big ones, are no match for persistent, hard work. That is how roads through mountains and pyramids were built. Our manual is a small example of that same phenomenon.

Me as Me (My Career)

One of the products we inspected was a one-time-use plastic device with a spring-loaded blade to draw a drop of blood used for testing. Some of the blades did not seem as sharp as we expected when viewed with a microscope. The manufacturer was Kestrel in Alabama. My boss and I got on the company Learjet at Morristown Airport about 8 a.m. and flew to Kestrel to inspect the product we'd purchased from them. We reviewed the manufacturing and inspection processes and resolved the problem. When we were done, the owner of the company invited us to his house for lunch. We had freshly killed, southern fried chicken that his wife had made for us. It was delicious. It actually tastes different from the chicken we normally eat. We got back on the company jet and were home for dinner. I still find it hard to believe that I had lunch in Alabama and dinner at home in New Jersey. What a country!

As supervisor, I was expected to write the reviews for all my employees. I found the group leader, Mike Donovan, to be extraordinary. Because of his years of experience, he knew how to handle every situation. He was tactful but frank with the inspectors and, overall, did an excellent job. I wrote his review reflecting these qualities. It seems that there was a committee that handed out raises that were tied to the review. The committee said he was an average employee and that, therefore, he should receive an average review. My boss asked me to rewrite the review to indicate that Mike was an average employee. I said if the committee thought Mike was average, let them write his review. I refused to change it. Weeks went by, and I was told that I was responsible for holding up Mike's raise. So, I sort of gave in. I rewrote the review indicating that Mike was average. However, at the bottom of the review, I stated, in bold print, "THIS REVIEW IS THE OPINION OF THE COMMITTEE AND DOES NOT REFLECT THE VIEW OF HIS IMMEDIATE SUPERVISOR." Mike did receive an average raise, but disobeying my boss was not looked at kindly. This seemed to be turning into a pattern for me. I knew that, eventually, I had to be self-employed.

Financial Advisor Beginnings

Charlie Roach, the person who suggested that we look at the house we bought on Sanford Drive, was an insurance agent who also sold mutual funds. Savia already had an Oppenheimer mutual fund and some individual stocks when I met her. The topic seemed interesting, and I wanted to learn more. Charlie invited me to visit his office and speak to some of the people there. There were eight part-time investment representatives in the office. Most were schoolteachers, and one managed the pension fund for a pharmaceutical company. What they all had in common was trying to provide supplemental income for their families. There were some general discussions on how mutual funds worked, but I could not go further until I was licensed.

In 1978, the owner of Intercontinental Securities, Mark Feldman, had just introduced a new product. It was an investment in portable phones. He said that, since this was not a security, I did not need a license to sell it. A person would buy a set of portable phones. The payment would be $10,000 for three months. At the end of the three months, your principal was returned with 10% interest ($1,000). 10% in three months was a very good deal but did seem risky. So the sponsor added another level of comfort for the investor. If the sponsor was unable to return the principal and make the 10% payment, he

Me as Me (My Career)

purchased a surety bond that guaranteed the investor would be paid. There were seminars with well-known celebrities promoting this amazing investment.

I started by making a list of everyone I knew — friends, family, and acquaintances. Investors couldn't get enough. When their three months were up, and they received their principal back with the 10% interest, they became even more excited and invested $20,000, $40,000, even $100,000 for the next three months. After a year and a half, everything was running smoothly — until it didn't. The checks stopped coming in. The obvious question is, "What about the bond?" There was no bond. It was a fraud from the start. It was a "Ponzi Scheme." The people who invested first were paid by the people who invested later, and those people were paid by the people who came after them, until there were not enough people to pay everyone who came before them. All of us were in shock. We had lost substantial amounts of our friends' and families' money. We did make a commission on the sale of the investment, but because we believed in it, it was also invested and lost, and now we had to pay an attorney to defend ourselves. The Securities and Exchange Commission (SEC) came to investigate and determined that this was indeed a security, so I was in extra trouble, since I did not have a license to sell securities.

One of the sales agents I was with had heard of an attorney, Harry Sears, in Mountain Lakes, who'd represented President Richard Nixon during his re-election campaign. He was our man. I think it was easy for him to understand that we had been duped, or we would not have put our own money and the commissions we had earned into this investment if we'd known it was a fraud, but we still had to pay him to prove this. It was a difficult time, with many sleepless nights. I even ended up in the Morristown Memorial Hospital with chest pains. While I was there, I asked if I could see Joanne Martin, whom I had worked with 10 years earlier in the lab at Warner Lambert. She had become a respected cardiologist and stopped in to visit and see how I was doing. No problem was found, and I was released.

I voluntarily contributed everything I had — $2,500 — to help recover the money that was lost. After many court battles and depositions, the investors received 10% of the money they had lost.

My career as a financial advisor seemed doomed to failure even before it started. Seven of the eight advisors who went through this with me resigned and returned to their full-time jobs. In November 1979, I left Intercontinental Securities and joined Cardell and Associates while I was still working at Warner Lambert full-time.

Joe Joshi, the pension manager who was recognized in *Who's Who in Finance,* and I became friends as we had struggled through that Com-Link fiasco together. Joe encouraged me to attend some Cardell meetings to become familiar with the industry terms and language. I was fortunate in that Warner Lambert allowed me to take my two weeks' vacation in half-day increments. That is how I spent most of my vacation. The meetings were about private-placement investments and involved tax savings. In one of the investments, called Epic, you could invest in highly leveraged real estate and receive a tax credit for five times the investment amount. It really did not matter how the investment did.

Through all the research I had done — every week I would go to the library and look at Valueline reports to see how the funds were doing — I mostly used Templeton Funds. They

Me as Me (My Career)

appeared to have excellent returns with relatively low risk. At Cardell, there was a bin where you would pick up a duplicate copy of mutual fund statements your clients received. One month, I would pick up my reports but noticed that most of the other reps were using Oppenheimer funds. The next month, MFS funds were predominant, and the next month Fidelity Advisor funds. I asked what was going on. It seems the different fund companies would run promotions and pay the rep extra for that month if you used their funds. Boy, was I naïve. I thought the reps would do what was best for the client.

I was still working at Warner Lambert, and Savia and I were supervisors in Shaklee, educating people and selling nutritional products, but I felt that an investment advisor was what I wanted to be. The problem was that I had just burned friends, family, and everyone I knew. Where would my clients come from? Joe Joshi thought we could do the tax returns for Shaklee distributors. They were all self-employed people with a special tax situation that I was familiar with, since I was also a distributor. That was the game plan. The problem was that I did not know how to do taxes, and Joe only knew the theory behind taxes. He knew that you could deduct expenses for an office in the home. You could deduct inventory, travel expenses, and more. What he did not know is how to record that on the tax forms. Joe went from Shaklee Office to Shaklee Office, where we met some big producers, and Joe gave talks to their people explaining how they were missing out on valuable deductions and paying too much in taxes. We could fix all that by doing their taxes for them. This is how I learned to do taxes. (Throw him in the water, and he will learn how to swim.)

I developed a booklet I gave to clients to help them know what expenses to keep track of. This is also how I obtained my investment clients. There was one master producer in Ohio who wanted to fly me in to do the taxes for his group and fly me back. Joe said I could call him and that he would talk me through the returns. He was a very persuasive person, but that was ridiculous. I did not go. Joe and I went on investment appointments together. He did most of the talking while I was learning the business. If they had all stocks, he said they should have bonds; if they had all bonds, they should have stocks. He could make a rational case for anything. Looking back on the situation, he was probably right. They should have some of both.

Job Change

My full-time, real job at Warner Lambert was changing. My division was moving to North Carolina. There was a job waiting for me there if I wanted to go. I had heard of previous moves where the new job unexpectedly ended in one year. Besides, my family was in New York, so I was not moving. I took my severance and, in September of 1982, I started New Horizons Financial Services. When I left Warner Lambert, they sent me to a career counselor. I took a test to see what profession I would be good at. Stockbroker came out horrible; Insurance Agent — horrible; Attorney — horrible; Salesman — horrible; Accountant — horrible. The term "Financial Advisor" or "Financial Planner" wasn't even a word back then! The test was accurate. I would not be good at any of those careers. What makes being a Financial Advisor so attractive to me is that you have to know about all these areas and then know when to call in the experts. Your knowledge base keeps changing and never gets dull. However, funnily enough, I did score very well as a Forest Ranger. I do like trees and nature.

Me as Me (My Career)

I was a Financial Advisor who made house calls. That was how business was conducted at the time. One way I could distinguish myself from other advisors was to be punctual. When I told someone I would be at their house at 7:30 p.m., I considered this a promise. I was not there at 7:25 or 7:40 — I was there at 7:30 p.m., exactly as I had promised. I thought this gave me the appearance of being organized, disciplined, a person of my word, a person of integrity, and someone who was considerate about their time. One client had a grandfather clock right by her front door. I would always ring her bell as the clock was chiming. I started with — at least — reliability in my favor. When you are late for an appointment, it appears that you do not have respect for the other person's time and are unorganized, and the ability to keep your word may be in question.

I was struggling and thought if I added insurance to my tool bag, it would increase my income. I asked the head of the Securities Firm, Frank Cardell, who I could talk to about insurance, and he referred me to Charlie Tomaro, the head of Tomorrow's Financial Services. They did investments and life insurance. I'd had a difficult time learning from Joe, since there were no foundational concepts. At Tomorrow's Financial Services, there was an investment philosophy that would help you choose a product for a client. They also had a philosophy regarding the type of life insurance to have, along with scripts to be used to explain the concepts to clients. This was exactly what I was looking for. At the time, I had left my $45,000/year job, Savia left her job to be a stay-at-home mom, and I was making $15,000 a year. I knew this is what I wanted to do — design plans to help people and make them more financially secure.

But could I support my family? I had few people to talk to and was considering bagging groceries at Shoprite. Savia encouraged me to continue with my "career." We converted our one-car garage into my home office by putting up a wall in the garage with just enough room to fit my ride-on lawn mower. A $1,000 client investment, significant at the time, would result in a commission to me of about $70. How could anyone in that profession survive? When I met with Charlie Tomaro and his wife, Rita, at their home, I said I would be happy if I could make $50,000 a year. Charlie laughed. He said that using his system, my income should far exceed that amount. I was willing to try. I had nothing to lose. It couldn't get any worse. I tried his system but had only a minor increase in income. Charlie suggested that, although I was receiving 100% of the commission, I could do better by giving up half of my commission to someone who would train me. He had offered this opportunity many times in the past to other reps, but nobody had ever accepted his offer. I would be the first. Don McDermott would be my trainer. I was put in with a group of his agents practicing and learning client scripts.

As a result of changing jobs, the Com-Link phone disaster, little income, and two small children and a wife to support, I ended up with severe fatigue. I went to many doctors, none of whom could determine the cause of my problem. The first two hours of every day was the only time I had any energy. The rest of the day, I had to rest in bed. I worked by speaking with the husband and wife, which usually took place in the evening, when both were home. This was no longer possible for me. The only other time I could see clients was on Saturday morning, when I had enough energy to seem normal. This went on for one year. Surprisingly,

Me as Me (My Career)

that year was one of my highest income-producing years. It seems focus is important. Apparently, what used to take me every night and Saturday morning, I could accomplish in just Saturday morning, if pressured.

With all my usual avenues of treatment exhausted, as I was, I went to see Dr. William Kelly, a chiropractor and homeopath. He easily determined that I had Epstein-Barr Virus (EBV), which had attacked my adrenal glands. He asked me to go for a blood test to confirm his hypothesis, and indeed, he was correct. He gave me a regime of homeopathic remedies and herbs and said it would help. After a year, the EBV was under control but not completely. Since then, I have had to take a nap every afternoon to get through the day.

A few years later, I ended up in the hospital with chest pains. A full array of tests could not find anything wrong, although I had a mitral-valve prolapse, which occurs in 2% of the population and is not usually a big deal. The doctor prescribed Enderol, a heart medication, to reduce the chances of the chest pains returning. I took this medication for the next five years, along with Nitroglycerin tablets in my pocket in case the chest pains returned. I was constantly tired and weak, and I had hot flashes. An aspirin seemed to help. So, I took one before every client appointment. There were several times when I had to excuse myself from the appointment and go home to rest.

I went to see Dr. Lev, another cardiologist, for guidance. He said the Enderol was causing these symptoms and that I did not have a heart problem. *Hallelujah!* He was right. I now needed only the afternoon nap. Fine by me. Both of these health issues happened during my thirties, and I'm thrilled to have them behind me.

Appointment with Marlene 1984

In the early 1980s, I was still working with Tomorrow's Financial Services. Some of the people in this firm were doing much better than I was and were willing to train me. The founder asked if I would be interested in going on a business appointment with his daughter, Marlene, as an observer, to see how their firm presented and explained their program to clients. This seemed like a great opportunity for me to learn from the top of the organization.

We were to meet at the Howard Johnson's restaurant at exit 129 off the Garden State Parkway at 7:30 p.m. The evening began normally. I left my house so that I would reach our meeting place on time. I could see the Howard Johnson's as I approached the tollbooth. I asked the toll attendant how to get to Howard Johnson's from there. He said I should have gotten off the exit before this. I would have to go to the next exit, get back on the Parkway in the opposite direction, go back two exits, and get off at exit 128. This would take about 30 minutes. It was already 7:30, and I didn't know if Marlene would wait until 8:00 for me (this was before cell phones). I asked if I could leave my car at the tollbooth where the toll collectors park. He said that would be OK — but only for 15 minutes. I agreed and started to walk toward the restaurant. When you are driving, it doesn't seem that important that it is raining, but when you are walking, in a suit, the rain is a little annoying. As I approached the restaurant, I noticed there was a fence surrounding the building. I weighed my choices.

Me as Me (My Career)

1. Walk back to my car, miss the appointment, have Marlene wait for me, and possibly be late for her appointment, or

2. Climb the fence.

I climbed the fence.

As I approached Marlene's car, I noticed that she was anxious about something. She said that she was glad to see me but also that we had to hurry, because the client lived far from our meeting spot. I told her we had to get back on the Parkway and pick up my car first. Then, we could leave my car off and drive together to the client's home. She agreed. She dropped me off to get my car, and we drove separately until we got off the Garden State Parkway. We parked my car and went together in her car. She drove.

What a coincidence — our appointment was for 8:00 p.m., and it was now 8:00 p.m., and we were lost. We were in the right part of the state, the northwest corner of New Jersey, but that was no help. That part of the state was not very populated. It was dark and wooded. We saw the lights of a house up ahead and pulled up to the house to ask for directions. As Marlene walked to the house, two large dogs attacked her. While she was yelling, the homeowner came out and quieted the dogs. Marlene was OK. He gave us directions as best he could. Eventually, we found the house. It was in a town called Ringwood.

It was now 10:00 p.m., and we were two hours late for our appointment. Marlene apologized for our tardiness and asked if it would be alright if we could start at this late hour. It was fine with them. Usually it takes two or three visits to explain all the details of a financial plan to a client. Marlene had driven four hours to get there, and she did not want to return anytime soon, so we went straight through until 2:00 a.m. Her plan and the presentation were excellent, but 2:00 a.m. was ridiculous.

As we left the house, I could see that Marlene was deliriously tired. She could barely keep her eyes open.

I offered to drive. As we left the house, I noticed a flashing light on the dashboard. We were running out of gas. I didn't know if the indicator light had just begun to signal us of impending doom or if it was flashing before we'd arrived at the client's house.

I was driving in a cold sweat, expecting to run out of gas any second. It was 2:30 in the morning. There were no lights on. We didn't know where any gas stations were or if they were open. Even if we could find a phone booth, which we couldn't, where would we say we were? We didn't know. At around 3:00 a.m., we found a gas station that was open. Perhaps gliding down hills in neutral helped.

Once the gas tank was filled, it felt like a weight had been lifted off our shoulders. Marlene had to use the bathroom, so we stopped at an all-night diner. While she was in the stall, she was surprised to see that there was no toilet paper. She asked the girl in the next booth to hand her some paper. The girl sounded drugged and said that she would be over to help Marlene when she was finished. Marlene didn't want help. She wanted toilet paper. This made Marlene very suspicious and nervous. She ran out of the diner, and we sped away. What type of people do you expect to be in a diner at 3:30 in the morning? Not normal people!

Me as Me (My Career)

Finally, we were on our way home. There was still one problem. Neither of us could remember where we had parked my car. Marlene was so tired that she didn't care. She said, "Don't worry. I'll buy you a new car. Let's go home." After a little more searching, we did find my car.

I arrived home at 4:30 a.m., while Marlene got home at 6:00 a.m. Our spouses were wondering what had happened to us. It didn't seem possible that we could explain the situation without us being in trouble.

I am not sure why, but no one ever went out on an appointment with Marlene again.

It would take a few more years before I was competent and started earning a reasonable income. For every prospecting call I made, I knew how many would become clients and the average amount I would make. Every December, Savia and I would get together and determine what our income goal should be for the next year. We called it "Dialing Your Income." If you want to make "X" income, then you need to make "Y" prospecting calls. The formula was simple. Its execution was not.

Don McDermott explained that, if you wanted to cut off a dog's tail, would you cut one piece at a time or cut the whole thing at once? This meant that, instead of making calls every day, it was better to make all the calls at once, on Friday night. The dreaded Friday night would come, and I forced myself to make the calls. You were supposed to stop when you had six appointments for the next week. I couldn't take that much abuse, so I would talk myself into saying that they were not home from work yet or that it was too late or too early until the calling window was closed. It was torturous. I can still feel the sweat through the memories.

Once a successful appointment had been made, then the job began. There were no cell phones or GPS navigation systems. Almost all appointments were at night, since that was when both the husband and wife were available. I asked the prospective clients for directions, but they were not always clear. Therefore, I had a street map of almost every county in New Jersey. Many times, I was lost and couldn't call to ask for clarification of directions or to tell them I would be late. I spent significant time on the side of the road at night, trying to read the map and the street signs, and trying to figure out where I was. I had a policeman's flashlight with me (Mag Lite) that could be used as a club, and, with a twist of the lens, I could zoom in to focus on a house number or street sign. There were times when I was two hours late for an appointment. Every year, I would go to this one particular client's house at night. Then, one year, they called me and said they had the day off, so I could see them during the day. I was so accustomed to driving to their house at night that I couldn't find it during the day. This was how I worked from my home office for the first 20 years of my career.

Even though I desperately needed income, I had an unusual attitude. My goal was, surprisingly, not to make the sale. Before every client meeting, I said a prayer to give me wisdom and guidance. Since I really believed my plans could significantly improve the clients' lives, my goal was to make the most persuasive presentation for my plan through education. If the plan was not accepted, *they* were the ones I felt would suffer.

Around 1996, Merrill Lynch (I think it was them) changed the entire retail-investment-management industry. At that time, all representative income was transaction driven. If you sold

Me as Me (My Career)

a product, you were paid upfront for the sale. Merrill Lynch pioneered a different concept. If we could provide ongoing management to an account, we would not be compensated upfront but continuously. You would sell a management program once, and, then, by providing ongoing management and monitoring, you would continue to be paid.

This changed the entire industry. Instead of scrambling for client transactions — an inherent conflict of interest — you could now get paid for managing and maintaining a *relationship*. I knew this was a great benefit to the investment advisor, but the question that remained for me was, *Did it benefit the client?*

Merrill Lynch's managed account consisted of dividing a portfolio into three categories — a portion in stock funds, a portion in bond funds, and a portion in cash. Every three months, these portions would be adjusted (rebalanced) back to the original percentages. This was an advantage. You could avoid ending up with an overly aggressive portfolio that was more heavily invested in stock funds than you wanted, but was it worth 1% to 2% per year? I didn't think so. If I was going to be involved in a managed account, it had to add more value and be worth the fee.

As a principal at TFS Securities, Inc., I managed other financial advisors. Two advisors in my group were dabbling in momentum-based portfolio management. This looked promising and a way to earn a fee for a managed account. I learned as much about it that I could. I met with the two advisors every week. We started using a program called Fasttrack, developed by an actual rocket scientist, that used artificial intelligence to read trends and project when to buy or sell a fund based upon momentum, relative strength, and moving average. It was fascinating and addictive. I joined a group that used the program and met monthly in Manhattan. That is where I met Susan Jeffrey, who had her own advisory firm and had been using momentum-based portfolio management for many years. The two advisors I spoke about did not fare so well. One thought his trading system was so wonderful that he no longer had clients but just managed his own money. The other advisor, previously very successful became addicted, thinking he could now read stock charts, put all his clients in an individual stock and bought and sold it as the charts and news swayed him. He lost his clients, his business, his house, and his wife. A difficult lesson to learn.

In 1997, I brought my Momentum Based Managed account to the head of TFS, Charlie Tomaro and Tom Hyland, who gave me the go-ahead to be the only proprietary managed account at TFS. It was called Dynamic Asset Allocation. Eventually, I collaborated with Susan Jeffrey in managing the program. There were five different models, based upon risk level. We used data from the past to design a trading system and married it with current data to arrive at our "optimized" system. Each night, the closing prices of all mutual funds were loaded into our program and were run to determine if we needed to make any trades. This happened every trading day, whether on vacation, sick, or dead. About once each year, all the trading systems needed to be reoptimized, as if starting new, because the systems became stale.

At the beginning, these systems worked well, and then, over time, fund companies did not like the short-term trades, so they imposed trading restrictions like fund minimum holding periods or redemption fees. Then the SEC jumped on board. You could not trade more than 10% of the 30-day average daily volume. The systems looked good but were labor intensive, and the trading restrictions seriously hampered the trading system and dragged down performance enough that, by 2012, I closed the program.

In 2005, the AIM Family of Mutual Funds introduced a software program that used a Nobel Prize-winning concept called Modern Portfolio Theory. Using this concept, I developed the Buy/Hold Plus managed account program that year. If you do the math, you will see that the two programs overlapped for about seven years. It was never-ending work, but I loved it.

In the year 2000, I was speaking to a person on our softball team who was considering renting space in Cedar Knolls, and he asked me if I would consider moving out of my home office and renting space from him. He owned a Property Casualty Agency (ADP) and said we could cross-sell to each other's clients. Having administrative staff in our house when we were not home would be a problem. It was time to move the business out of the house and start a "real" company. We worked together for 20 years, and the cross-selling never happened. Also, at that time, my daughter Tara became a Registered Representative with TFS Securities, and I did not want her going to prospects' or clients' homes unaccompanied. Savia was great at converting my house-call business to a meet-at-the-office business. I am not sure how she pulled that off, but she's one of those people who can accomplish the impossible. Daria worked with Savia, performing all the necessary administrative work and was the go-to person for all insurance-related items. In 2005, Daria left to take on an important role as full-time mother, while Tara continued to work with us. Imagine working together with your wife and children every day. That would be a nightmare for many families. But to us, it was a blessing.

Barbara Ricciardi, who had worked for another agent I supervised, was between jobs and heard that there was an opening with us. She was a perfect fit — conscientious, experienced, and honest. Her son, Chris, worked for us as an intern a few years later. The workload was becoming more than I could handle. Also, I was getting older, and we needed a continuity/succession plan for the business and clients we had built up over the years. Joe Okaly was the answer to this prayer. He is what I would call a "Renaissance Man." He has the attitude that you are limited only by the limits you put on yourself. An inspiring attitude to have. How did he come to work at New Horizons? Barbara knew him from her neighborhood, and he played with her kids growing up, but she did not refer him. Chris was Joe's longtime friend and college roommate, but he did not refer him, either. The owner of one of the offices I managed heard that Joe, whom she did not know, was looking for an internship, and that is how we met. After observing him as an intern, I offered him a job when he graduated, which he accepted. Was it a coincidence that Joe and Barbara came to work with us? I don't think so.

TFS Conventions 1985 to 2009

The higher-level producers at TFS would be rewarded with an all-expenses-paid company trip each year. These would be considered world-class trips by any measure. We were encouraged to take our children along, although we paid for them. This was a way for the next generation to meet each other and form long-term bonds.

Me as Me (My Career)

Our first trip was to **Seattle** in 1985. We took a boat to The Long House, where we watched as smoked salmon was prepared. This was the first time anyone in my family had had salmon — and after that, it was added to our regular meals. Daria and Tara loved riding up and down the escalator in the hotel. It's fun at any age.

Prior to leaving for another TFS convention, this time in **Barbados,** I had a scab on my elbow that I continued to pick at, so by the time I reached the island, it was swollen and infected. They should make elbow covers for this in the same way they make collars for dogs to prevent them from scratching themselves — or maybe a Band-Aid would have helped. The hotel recommended a doctor on the island. Savia and I arrived by taxi to a one-level, two-room house about 15 feet by 20 feet. It was the middle of the summer, about 120 degrees inside with no air conditioning. It was normal housing for Barbados but something I was not accustomed to. There were about five other patients ahead of me. By the time it was my turn, I was covered in sweat. I lay down on the examining table next to the wall, as instructed by the doctor. As the needle without anesthethics went into my elbow to drain the fluid, my legs climbed up and down the wall while I was screaming in pain. I am sure the poor patients after me were reconsidering the necessity for their doctor visit. Crisis averted — or was *that* the crisis? When I arrived home, I intended to send the doctor an air conditioner in gratitude but never followed through. For the special event, our transportation was a pirate ship, which included an interactive show consisting of some of our friends walking the plank into the ocean.

On another convention, TFS rented an island for us in the **Bahamas,** where we spent the day playing and snorkeling.

On **Grand Cayman Island,** TFS arranged some beach activities for us. During one event, there were 4 teams. Each team member had to run 50 yards, drink a large glass of alcoholic juice, run back 50 yards, spin around 10 times with your forehead on the top of a crutch with the bottom in the sand, and then run back 50 yards to the finish line. When it was my turn, I ran the 50 yards, but instead of drinking the alcoholic juice, I threw it on my tee shirt, thinking it would make me more stable. I ran back 50 yards, put my forehead on the crutch, and started my first spin. I forgot to mention: I get dizzy easily. Before I finished my first turn, I fell, knocking down the team next to me, and creating one big domino effect, with all four contestants falling down. I got up, still dizzy, and, instead of running back to the finish line, I ran right into the water. We were laughing for weeks. TFS took movies of this and played it regularly at the home office to viewers who were predictably, hysterical. When I arrived home, I began "Fountain of Youth" exercises by Peter Kelder and continued every day for four years. This cured my dizziness! Better late than never.

While on a TFS **Bermuda** convention, we decided to rent mopeds to tour the island. We went together to the rental place with our good friends Don and Madeline. We each had a bike. By each, I mean Don, Madeline, Daria, and Tara, while Savia and I shared a bike. The sun had set, and we were riding back at night to the hotel from the city of Hamilton. Savia and I led the group, followed by Daria and Tara, and then Don and Madeline. Savia and I rode over a hill and proceeded down the other side. Our bike stopped at the bottom of the hill and would not start. We waited for the others to join us, but that didn't happen. We wondered why they were not with us. We

Me as Me (My Career)

knew they were OK since they were with Don and Madeline, but that wasn't acceptable to Savia, the mom. What happened to them? Where were they? Why did our bikes stop? Savia was in a state of panic and anger knowing that her children were on the island at night without us.

After about 15 minutes had passed, we saw them walking their bikes down the hill. It was then that we realized that we had all run out of gas at the same time. All of us walked our bikes to a phone booth, a considerable distance away. Although this was after hours, Savia called the phone number of the bike-rental owner to complain about us not having enough gas and being stranded. We didn't think the conversation would go too well in her present state, so Don spoke to the owner. First, we had to calm Savia, since our goal was to have the owner's cooperation in getting us back to the hotel — not complaining about running out of gas. Eventually, the owner came with gas cans and refilled our tanks, so we could return to the hotel. Years later, I was speaking with another person on the trip discussing our Bermuda convention, and he said he remembered seeing Savia yelling and screaming in the middle of the street and thought she was drunk. I guess that was during the height of her anger, frustration, and worry about her children. Moral: it all works out in the end (or check your bike's gas tank when renting).

> "Everything will be okay in the end.
> If it's not okay, it's not the end."
> — *Fernando Sabino but often quoted by Robert Giarraffa*

At the **Turnberry Isle** convention in Florida, my parents came along. By coincidence, the Chicago Bulls basketball team was there at the same time. When my father, age 75, got into the elevator with the team, he said his brother was a big fan of theirs and asked if he could get an autograph. Seeing right through him, they asked, "How old is your brother?" He felt a little foolish saying his brother was 67, so he said "13." which was equally foolish. They looked at him in disbelief but gave him the autograph, which he gave to his brother, Mike.

At every TFS convention there was always one day that required a tuxedo. On **Paradise Island,** the guys were hanging around at the pool after dinner, when the group, led by the company founder, became rowdy. He started pushing his associates into the pool with their tuxedos on, including Leonard, who wore a toupee. It was an amusing sight to see Leonard on one side of the pool and his toupee floating on the other side.

There was a band playing outside the restaurant where we ate that night. After dinner, we noticed that the band had left for break. One of our associates, Paul, decided we should take over their instruments and conduct a dance contest. Each of us were dancing in couples; Paul would come to a couple and decide they should be removed from the competition until only one couple was left. Fortunately, we finished our dance contest before the band returned.

For regulatory and financial reasons, 2009 was the last convention. It was great while it lasted. Moral: enjoy the present.

Me as We (Relationships and Married Life)

During the last year of high school, there was a dance I wanted to ask Mary Lou to. She was the girl from whom I'd borrowed *The Legend of Sleepy Hollow* in elementary school; she lived around the block from me in Brooklyn. During high school, you did not go on solo dates. It was always a double date. She asked if she could bring her friend and if I would bring my friend. I invited my friend Kevin Gilbride on the double date, and Mary Lou brought her friend Peggy. As soon as I introduced Kevin, Mary Lou and he were seriously smitten. You could actually say it was "love at first sight." Peggy was not my first choice, but I liked her, and my first choice was taken.

We went on many double dates together, and our feelings for each other grew. Peggy lived with her mother, since her father had passed away while at church when she was a young child. I would see her on weekends. We would either go out, mostly on double dates with Kevin and Mary Lou, or we would sit in her living room, listening to Jean Shepherd

A Blessed and Guided Life

tell stories of his childhood on the radio while Peggy's mother also listened in the next room.

The four of us went to Wolf's Pond on Staten Island for a picnic. I drove, since I was the only one with a driver's license. I pulled the 1956 Ford up to a row of bushes while we picnicked on the beach. When we got into the car to leave, the car would not go in reverse. So, through the bushes we went. On the way back, it started to rain. I turned the windshield wipers on but still couldn't see too well. As we approached the toll booth for the Verrazano Bridge, my windshield wiper blade flew off and slingshot about 30 feet into the air. We were all hysterical, and now I could see even less.

I also drove the four of us to the senior prom. It was a big deal. We all got dressed up to go. When Kevin rolled down

Me as We (Relationships and Married Life)

the back window, it came off the track, and we spent a while "fishing" it out with a metal clothes hanger. What a great car!

One year, Peggy became sick, and her aunt Alice, who lived on a horse farm in Green Village, New Jersey, helped out. Peggy went to Morristown Memorial Hospital for treatment.

Is it a coincidence that, years later, my two daughters live three minutes from Green Village and were both born in Morristown Memorial Hospital? I don't believe in coincidences.

I went out with Peggy all through college. However, after five years, it was over.

Kevin was a great guitar player who made it look easy, so I thought I should learn to play. I took lessons from Mr. Lipari, about two miles from my house, for about three years. Even though most of the time I did not practice at home but only played at the lesson itself, Mr. Lipari suggested that I teach guitar to other students, but I never felt that confident. I could have been so much better. That was foolish. However, I did practice during class in high school. Kevin and I would place rubber bands lengthwise along our 12-inch wooden rulers to practice our strums.

Meeting Savia

I did not realize that my cousin's wife, Fran, was waiting for the opportunity to introduce me to her friend from work. Word of my breakup with Peggy got around, and Fran was ready to try her matchmaking skills.

My cousin Bernard was having difficulty passing his chemistry exam, and since I majored in chemistry in college, I thought I could help. I went to his home in Brooklyn near Erasmus High School and began tutoring him. His wife,

Fran, was always there, making me feel at home and feeding us. Bernard did well on his test, and, as payment, he would set me up on a blind date with Fran's girlfriend, with whom she worked at Pfizer in Manhattan. I had never been on a blind date before but had heard horror stories and wasn't expecting much.

It was Saturday, August 10, 1968, and I was driving my friend Kevin to the submarine base in Groton, Connecticut, to report in for service in the Navy. It was a three-hour car ride one way. We left early on that beautifully clear day. It was a relaxed, pleasant ride. Kevin and I spoke about his upcoming stint in the Navy and what he might experience. We also discussed my blind date for that evening. Neither one of us knew what we were getting into. There was a little more traffic than I had expected, and the chances of me being on time for my 6:00 p.m. blind date were fading fast. I am always on time. It is part of who I am.

I got home, ate, dressed, and left for Fran and Bern's house, a half-hour away. I arrived uncharacteristically late, 6:10 p.m. When I walked in, I was introduced to Savia. Just the name sounded exotic. She was wearing a white blouse and tight white shorts, and she had curly, short, brown hair and a summer-sun dark tan. This blind date far exceeded my expectations. I don't know how I looked to her, but my cousin Bern said I was so thin that I had to run around in the shower to get wet. We all spoke for a while and then decided to go to Jahn's, an ice-cream shop in the area.

We all got in Bern's "van" for the ride to Jahn's. Bern is not what you would call an ordinary, conventional type of person, and neither was his van. It was an old van, with two seats in the front for Fran and Bern. The back seats were missing, and

Me as We (Relationships and Married Life)

in their place was a wooden bench, which I assumed Bern had installed. On the floor of the van, there were many areas where you could see through to the road below, since the floor was missing. This is where Savia and I sat.

Bern did his best to constantly swerve the van, so that Savia and I would be forced to help each other stay seated. I didn't mind. We finally arrived at Jahn's and ate a ton of ice cream. The night was over, and we went our separate ways; however, I knew I would see her again.

My First Official Date

My first "official" date with Savia was two weeks later, on a Thursday night. I asked her to the Westbury Music Fair on Long Island to see Andy Williams, the singer. My parents were eager to meet her but decided it was too early in the relationship. As we were driving to Westbury, I noticed my family passing by in another car and craning their necks to

get a look at my date. During intermission, we stood up to stretch our legs and look around, and I saw my family seated many rows behind us. Were they there to see Andy Williams or us? I still don't know. During our first few dates, Savia spoke very little. Was she shy, nervous, or sizing me up? It was just strange.

After years of searching, wondering, and false starts, was this the girl I would end up with? I didn't know. The next time I saw Savia was when I was invited to her house for Sunday lunch to meet her family. She lived at 45-38 48th Street in Woodside, Queens, about a 30-minute drive from my house in Brooklyn. Savia lived with her two brothers, Carl and Dario, in a six-unit apartment house her parents owned. Her father, Dario, and brother-in-law Angelo owned their own business, making display units for department stores from a loft in Manhattan. He also submitted the design for the "Space Shuttle" to the Patent Office in Washington D.C. He was a genius and spent many years of his life developing a safety device for airplanes. Savia's father also had played the accordion on radio every week when he was in his twenties. Savia's mother, Nina, had lived through the Great Depression and learned to be very thrifty. She would see beautiful dresses and coats in nice stores and go home to create her own pattern on paper bags and then make the clothing. She would buy day-old fruit at discount prices to save money. Carl had inherited musical talent from his father and was a self-taught lead guitarist in a band. Dario was the quiet brother whom everyone loved. He would ride his bike throughout the neighborhood and stop at all the pizza shops where the owner would give him free slices of pizza. This was also true of donut shops, etc. Dario loved food and telling one-liner jokes.

Me as We (Relationships and Married Life)

This was the family I would be marrying into.

We spent many hours driving around, averaging 500 miles each weekend. After we'd dated for about two years, we were engaged to be married. We also realized at the time that we needed another car. I had only recently started working and had little savings. Savia had started work earlier than I and had some funds saved. We decided to buy a new car, and Savia said she would pay for it—a little unorthodox, but who was I to argue? It was one of the first cars in America made in Japan. It was a white 1970 Toyota Corona Mark II with a black vinyl roof. The foreign cars had more conveniences and "bells and whistles" than the American cars had, and this one was an amazing bargain at only $2,500.

We were driving around one Saturday winter night near JFK airport in Queens. As part of our normal driving exploration, I drove down a narrow side street that had a steep decline. I didn't realize that the street was covered with a thin film of ice. The car kept sliding uncontrollably down the street, until it reached the end of the street, where the front of the car plunged head first into a lake. We were in shock and didn't even know there was a lake in Queens! The front tires of our car were submerged in the shallow lake water while the rear tires were on the icy road. After the tension of not being able to control the car and ending up in the lake, I had a chance to relax and observe the area around us. There were four or five other cars in exactly the same situation we were in. We all started laughing in response to our common problem.

Then, the next car was arriving as we all looked on, hoping it would not collide with one of our cars. Fortunately, it did not. I took the jack out of the car trunk and stepped into the icy water to see if I could level the car and (a little optimistically) back it out of the lake. Eventually, after knocking on many doors, we found someone who would call a tow truck for us. Each of the cars were towed out of the lake. When we arrived at Savia's house past her curfew, we told them our story.

After this incident, we bought snow tires with metal studs and tire chains. They really worked well. We used them every winter until they were outlawed in our town for tearing up the roads.

Savia

Savia's mother and father had gone to a play in Manhattan when her mother was pregnant with her. The princess in the play was named "Savia." They loved the name so much that they bestowed it on their first child. It was never clear what nationality the name came from until Savia and I were at Lord & Taylor department store and we noticed an

Me as We (Relationships and Married Life)

employee-of-the-month plaque indicating that a "Favia" was the winner in the women's clothing department. We had never heard the name "Savia" before and wondered if Favia had. It was a long shot, but worth a try. When we arrived at the women's clothing section, we found out that Favia had been reassigned to another department for the day. We had the entire store looking for Favia. When we finally found her, she said that in her country, Afghanistan, "Savia" was a popular name. Ah, ha! The name was Persian. It makes sense since her father's name, "Dario," is also Persian. Mystery solved.

I would like to borrow the lyrics from a song from the movie *The Sound of Music* that depicts the character in the lead role — Maria — but change the name to Savia. Here it is:

> How do you solve a problem like Savia?
> How do you catch a cloud and pin it down?
> How do you find a word that means Savia?
> A flibbertijibbet! A will-o'-the wisp! A clown!
> Many a thing you know you'd like to tell her
> Many a thing she ought to understand
> But how do you make her stay
> And listen to all you say
> How do you keep a wave upon the sand?
> Oh, how do you solve a problem like Savia?
> How do you hold a moonbeam in your hand?
> When I'm with her I'm confused
> Out of focus and bemused
> And I never know exactly where I am
> Unpredictable as weather
> She's as flighty as a feather

> She's a darling! She's a demon! She's a lamb!
> She'd out-pester any pest
> Drive a hornet from its nest
> She could throw a whirling dervish out of whirl
> She is gentle! She is wild!
> She's a riddle! She's a child!
> She's a headache! She's an angel!
> She's a girl!

When we got married, she made a pledge to herself to be the best wife and mother she could be, and I think she fulfilled her promise. There is no other person on the planet that I would want to spend my life with. She is the spirit behind everything I do. I thank Fran, Bern, and God for every day I have with her.

The Beginning of Our Life Together
Renting at 46 Dafrack Drive 1971–1973

Savia and I had our wedding reception at the Glen Terrace in Brooklyn on April 18, 1971 after dating for three years and honeymooned at The Sonesta in Bermuda. Since my job was in Morris Plains, New Jersey, we looked for a place in the area. We couldn't afford a house, so we began our life together in a garden apartment complex in Lake Hiawatha called "Knoll Gardens." We were at 46 Dafrack Drive. It consisted of a living room, kitchenette, and one bedroom. We were both working at Warner Lambert.

I was an average player on the company ping-pong team and needed more practice. We purchased a ping-pong table, but there wasn't much room for it in the apartment. We decided to put it in the living room, upon which the front door opened. You would have to squeeze your way past it to get to the rest of the apartment. Savia was a novice player, but after not-so-many hours of practice, we were equals. The first thing we did as soon as we got home was change our clothes and play ping-pong. We stayed there for two years until we had saved up enough to buy a house. During our weekend excursions through New Jersey, we became fascinated with Kinnelon. It had beautiful lakes throughout the town and seemed like the country atmosphere we were looking for. We looked for an empty lot to build on and had a deposit on a corner lot on Fayson Lake Road that we really liked. That area had no sewers, so you would have had to build a septic for the new home. The average cost of a septic at that time was $4,000, so since we really liked the lot, we put a contingency in the contract that any cost of more than $8,000 would be paid by the seller. We thought that was a reasonable request, however, the seller did not. The deal was dead. Fortunately, we did not let our emotions dictate the terms.

Our First House
Sanford Drive 1973–1990

Savia had a friend at work who said there was a house in Randolph that we should look at. It was a 1,300-square-foot split-level at 70 Sanford Drive. The first time we saw the house, we knew it was the one for us. It was barn red, with a one-car garage and a driveway that sloped up to the street. This house had three bedrooms and a bathroom upstairs, an eat-in kitchen, dining room, and living room on the first floor, and a TV room with a fish tank built into the wall downstairs. The fish tank did it for me. Our two years as apartment dwellers were over. The neighborhood consisted of all split-level homes arranged in a horseshoe configuration. There were many children playing outside, and the schools were rated highly. Our lawn was half an acre and took hours every week to mow, so I eventually bought a ride-on lawn mower.

My father was outside gardening and teaching my neighbors how to edge their lawns. He met the neighborhood. Then he introduced *me* to my neighbors.

When he went to my house or Loretta's, he would clean up, organize, fix things, and plant things — and not tell us. He wasn't looking for praise or even acknowledgement. He was just happy to help.

There was a 150-foot row of high, thorn-covered rose bushes that lined the side of our property, providing privacy for our house. Twice each year, Savia and I would change into our version of an "Ironman" outfit — tall boots, hat, goggles, gloves, and no visible skin — so we could trim the bushes. Even with all the preparation, the thorns had their way with us. My parents often came over during bush-pruning season to help us. When we'd been in the house for 12 years, we saw a contractor passing by with a backhoe. We hired him to pull out our bushes. It was either lose privacy or add scars. We chose the former.

There was no separation between our backyard and our neighbor's. We decided to add a row of pines as a natural border. Savia and I went to a farm and bought about 30 one-foot-tall pine trees. Savia's father, in his unique manner, installed the trees. Wearing his white shirt, tie, dress shoes and pants, he

Me as We (Relationships and Married Life)

cleared the area like a human backhoe. He was amazing and could do anything. No job was too big.

The fish tank was beautiful but also caused some problems. It was built into the wall, so you had to go down the basement steps to turn the fish-tank light on and feed the fish. Twice, the light fell into the tank, frying all the fish. Not a pleasant sight. Twice the heater malfunctioned and cooked the fish. I did not realize that male swordtail fish liked to jump out of the tank, so I had to add a cover. After sacrificing some fish, we eventually got the hang of it.

About once each year, we would thoroughly clean the fish tank. Both the fake and the real plants would be removed, along with the accessories, and the old water would be replaced with new, clean water. The first step, however, was to catch the fish and keep them in a temporary container during the transition. The fish were very adept at avoiding the net, not knowing what was in store for them. They didn't understand that the next place would be an improvement. It reminds me of us and the afterlife.

My cousins, aunts, and uncles would come to our house, where we would have birthday parties and celebrate holidays. One of our standard fun activities was Wiffle ball. Two captains would choose their teams, and the games would begin. It was a wonderful time to get together and create memories.

About every five years, Savia and I would paint the house after work and on weekends. The house was barn red with white trim. The front of the house faced south, resulting in cracked and peeled wooden planks above the garage. I would climb the ladder to the second story of the house and, using a hot iron we had rented, bake the paint off the wood and scrape it to prepare it for painting. After several hours each day of this activity, my forearms looked like Popeye's. When we finished painting the house, which took several weeks, Savia and I would sit in folding chairs in the driveway facing the house and admire our work. We were a little strange. Nothing's changed.

Besides painting, the house needed some improvements. We had a friend at work, George Ryals, who was very handy. Together, we built a seating area and cabinets for the kitchen, put a new roof on the house, and fixed the basement water problem by installing French drains around the perimeter of the basement. There was not much insulation in the attic. This was a job my father and I would tackle. We dressed in one-piece white paper suits over our clothes, wore a hat, goggles, and gloves, and added tape between our gloves and shirt sleeves, and between our shoes and pants. We didn't want any fiberglass on our skin. All this clothing made us sweat and fogged our goggles. Another challenge was where the attic floor met the roof. It was a small space we had to crawl into, staying mindful that the roof above us had roofing nails in it that were eager to see what the inside of our heads looked like. When we were done, we painted our names on the rafters in the attic to permanently leave our mark that we'd been there, sort of like what the astronauts did when they landed on the moon.

Young and Fearless
Extra Income

Savia and I were always looking for extra income. After all, we lived in America — so why not give it a shot and see what we could accomplish?

Me as We (Relationships and Married Life)

Pantyhose

My parents were never self-employed. They worked for companies or the city of New York. Savia's parents, on the other hand, were always self-employed. They were the entrepreneurs. We were sitting around the kitchen table one morning at Savia's parent's house when her mother brought out a newspaper containing an advertisement for buying pantyhose wholesale. She said we could buy them wholesale and sell them to people we knew at retail. Savia and I considered the idea. We met with the manufacturer in Manhattan and determined that we could buy these pantyhose at a deep discount. We bought them in bulk for $0.39 and could sell them for $0.99. The store price was about $2 per pair. This was our first attempt at entrepreneurship. It was exciting! Shortly thereafter, we were making frequent trips to Manhattan to pick up our order of pantyhose. Savia and I had just purchased, with her funds, a brand new 1970 Toyota Corona Mark II — white with a black vinyl top. It was beautiful. However, it was a relatively small car — we had no idea that we would be hauling boxes of pantyhose. The driver's seat would recline all the way back. We would load up the car with boxes and boxes of pantyhose so that you could see out of the driver's front window only. We would put the seat in the full-recline position. I would drive home from Manhattan, and Savia would sit behind me. It was a little dangerous, but then we were young and stupid. Savia worked at Pfizer in Manhattan, and I worked at Warner Lambert in Morris Plains, New Jersey. We would make deliveries to all the floors before work and at lunch. My sister, Loretta, made the deliveries at her workplace also. We made $3,000, which helped toward the down payment for our first house.

New Car Sales

Now that Savia and I had the self-employment fever, we were always looking for opportunities. The price of new cars was high, and the process of negotiating with the car dealerships was torturous. We found a company that would let us sell a car for $150 over cost. We went for training and started "Detroit Automotive Services." Because of the way car dealerships get paid, we made about $1,000 on each car we sold. Imagine buying a car for $150 over cost, with the option of picking it up at the dealers, picking it up yourself in Detroit, or, for $200 extra, having it driven from Detroit to your home. I think we sold only about three cars total, including a Pontiac Trans Am, but the experience was amazing.

Wicker Furniture

We liked wicker furniture and thought that it could possibly be our next venture by starting a wicker-furniture catalogue company. This furniture is made overseas, and its importation was something we were not familiar with. We made an appointment to speak to the Indian ambassador at the embassy in Manhattan. He discussed how it all worked and the import taxes involved. After our discussion, it was clear that this was not for us. When we left the embassy, we got into our car and noticed that the ambassador had just come out. We asked if he needed a ride somewhere. He accepted, and we took him to his next meeting.

Shaklee

Savia had read a book called *Tobey*. It was about how to improve your health by paying attention to what you eat. It

Me as We (Relationships and Married Life)

changed our lives. We were again looking for business opportunities when Savia noticed an advertisement at the YMCA to become involved with a Fortune 500 Company, distributing their products relating to health. It was a multi-level marketing company, educating people about natural vitamins and safe cleaning products. We learned about nutrition and marketing from our sponsor, Joyce Fitzgerald. We would invite many people to the weekly meeting at our house, but rarely would anyone show up. It was discouraging, but we persisted. Eventually we were selling a minimum of $3,000 in products each month, which qualified us as Supervisors, with company-paid trips. We would meet with different people, hear their story or ailment, and know which vitamins were appropriate to help them. I guess you could say we were practicing nutrition without a license. After a while, I could look at a person and know what their problem was before they spoke a word. Of course, our subsequent conversation would confirm my suspicions, and then we would proceed with the suggested regime of supplements. My aunt Tessie's diabetes level of 165 was reduced to a normal level of 125 by Shaklee vitamins. Another friend of mine had severe psoriasis and had tried all the doctor-prescribed medications. Gone in two weeks. I personally had a plantar's wart on the bottom of my foot that made it difficult to walk. It was cut out twice and frozen twice, but it kept coming back. Vitamins did the trick. I also wore reading glasses. The need for the glasses went away when I started taking vitamins, and I did not need glasses again until 10 years later. Natural vitamins did make a difference, and my anecdotal stories proved it, at least to me.

Real Estate Investments

Savia and I had a goal of owning a house in every state. We had two properties in Pennsylvania. We owned a piece of land in Saw Creek that we sold to buy our first house and were joint owners in a rental property in Easton with our supervisor from Shaklee and a common friend. We also owned two properties in Myrtle Beach, South Carolina. One was a newly built, beautiful townhouse, but because the area had been overbuilt, we sold it at a loss seven years later. We also owned a home on Hunters Lane. That is as far as we got in our "every state" goal. It was a great experience, and we learned a lot about real estate overall, but it was not a successful investment.

Making New Friends
Hawaii Trip

When you picture Hawaii, what does it look like? I picture beautiful isolated beaches, lush vegetation, palm trees, and a light wind.

In 1975, Savia and I went on vacation to Hawaii with my sister, Loretta, her husband, Frank, and my cousin John and his wife, Joanne. We got off the plane and were on a shuttle bus for about a 45-minute ride to our hotel on the island of Oahu. The view was not what I had expected. Honolulu was under construction. There were buildings in different stages of construction and piles of building materials everywhere. As we drove farther and farther from the airport, the scenery improved and did live up to its reputation. We were 5,000 miles from home and were eager to see this new part of the world. Our typical vacations are not for relaxing but for sightseeing.

Me as We (Relationships and Married Life)

Savia and I rented a car to see the island. We drove all over the island, stopping at a cafeteria-style place for lunch and visiting the Byodo-In Temple, a replica of a temple in Japan.

It was the first time we had seen this style of architecture in person. It was so open and peaceful that you could spend hours there doing nothing and be happy.

We were driving back to the hotel a little quickly because we were behind schedule. We had booked a sunset dinner cruise on a catamaran that evening. We boarded the catamaran, a boat with two hulls comprising the bottom, with a flat top for the passengers. Our sunset dinner cruise started in calm waters, where tropical drinks were served and Hawaiian music was being played. We were surprised that many of the tourists were Asian. Hawaii is a beautiful place, and it's as far from Asia as it is from the continental U.S. It was approaching sunset, and the ocean view was spectacular. The fun started when we were far away from land, where the ocean waters were not so friendly.

As the cruise continued, the waves became enormous, and the boat was bobbing up and down in the water. Many of the passengers were becoming nauseous. Savia was on the brink of being added to that number. I handed her some gum to distract her, along with every joke I could think of. It seemed to work. I looked around the boat and saw many people actually vomiting over the side. There was one Asian woman near us who was close to heaving. I smiled and gave her some gum, which appeared to help.

At this point, we turned around, and there was the crew attempting to serve dinner on lap tables. The scene was hysterical! The laughing helped with the nausea.

Fortunately, the boat headed back to port, where the waters were calmer.

We were back at our hotel in bed when we remembered that, if we wanted to see any of the other islands, tomorrow would be our only opportunity. The tour would leave at 5 a.m. We decided we were going, although we did not make reservations. At 4:30 a.m., we arrived at the designated departure point for the tour, taking our chances and realizing that we may not be able to go. The tour guide was very nice. However, it was his first day on the job. So, at 4:30 a.m., he called his supervisor and received approval to add us. We flew on a small plane to Hawaii, the big island, where we walked on a live volcano. On Kauai, there was a river cruise to the blue grotto. There were Americans and Asians lined up to board the boat, which was filling up fast. It was a flat-top boat with seats on each side. The Americans were on one side, and the Asians were on the other. When it was our turn to board, there were no more seats available. We saw someone on the Asian side rearranging people and waving to us. It was the Asian woman I had given the gum to the day before on the dinner cruise off Oahu. She had a friendly, smiley greeting for us. As the cruise started, the American side sang the national anthem, and the Japanese side sang their country's song. We were somewhere in between. Although we did not speak each other's language, when Savia and she were through, the Asian woman knew that we'd been married for four years and did not have children.

When the trip was over, we got together with the rest of the group to reminisce about Hawaii. We showed them the movies we took on the trip, and they were astounded. They kept saying, "I didn't see that." Loretta said, "I guess we'll have to go back to see it."

The scenery was beautiful and well worth the nine-hour plane flight.

The Right People for the Job?
Moving the Plane 1987

In 1947, Dario Manfredi and Vincent Burnelli were sitting in a coffee shop in lower Manhattan. The headline in the newspaper that day told of the accident of another plane that had just crashed, killing all the people aboard. Dario wondered if it was possible to install some safety device on all planes that would prevent crashes or save the passengers. He was not familiar with planes, since he was a self-taught cabinetmaker who supplied display furniture to department stores and managed his own real estate properties. Vincent Burnelli was a noted inventor of a new type of plane and had been recognized in *Who's Who in Aviation*. This was the right person for Dario to speak with. After a discussion with Vincent, Dario concluded that, if the fuselage of the plane (the part of the plane that holds the passengers) came down by parachute without the wings, the danger of fire would be eliminated since the fuel is stored in the wings. He designed a sprocket-and-gear system that would separate the wings from the fuselage simultaneously, and both would come down by parachute. He went to engineers at that time for a cost estimate to build his concept. He was shocked to find out that building his concept would cost a minimum of $1 million. This was in 1947. He decided that he would work on this project himself, due to financial constraints. Dario spent the next 37 years of his life toward achieving this goal.

There have been many chapters in the history of this project, including:

1. The FAA rewriting regulations in the National Register to permit the separation of an aircraft in flight. Before this landmark regulation, a coffee cup could not be released from an aircraft. Now the wings could be released.

2. The person who did the electrical work on the "L.E.M." for NASA's mission to the moon donating his time to help design and install the circuitry needed.

3. Many meetings with the Pentagon.

4. Threats from the family who'd developed the ejection seat.

5. Interview on the Barry Farber radio show.

After 20 years of effort, the prototype of Dario's concept was ready for a test run. On November 9, 1967, with 50-mph winds, his system proved to work successfully at Lakehurst Air Force Base in New Jersey.

The success of this flight was televised all over the world and was featured in *LIFE Magazine.*

In December 1984, with 90% of the project completed for certification and a meeting scheduled for the next day with

Me as We (Relationships and Married Life)

the FAA, Dario Manfredi passed away. This story relates the adventure encountered by Dario's son, Carl and me during the summer of 1987, while the plane was being moved to a different location.

The plane was located in a barn on Long Island. However, the lease had expired, and the plane needed to be moved. Dario and his wife, Nina, were thrifty people. It should have come as no surprise when Nina, Carl's mother, asked Carl and me if we could move the plane. It needed to be transported to a hangar about 30 miles from the barn, and the cost of hiring a firm to do this seemed high, since the family did most things themselves without much difficulty. I wondered if we were up to the task. This was the plane my father-in-law had worked on most of his life and could be an invention that would save many lives in the future. It was felt that this plane would possibly be on display at the Smithsonian Institute in Washington, D.C.

The responsibility we had accepted appeared enormous. Carl made preparations for the move. From an advertisement in the papers, Carl arranged to rent the pickup truck needed to transport the plane. The truck was in perfect condition. It was about one year old, highly polished, with a large bed we could tie the plane's wheels to. I left my home in New Jersey about 5:30 a.m. and arrived at Carl's house on Long Island about 6:30 a.m. We needed an early start, since we expected it to be a long day. Carl drove to the house where we were to pick up the truck. We rang the doorbell, and Pat, the truck's owner, came to the door. He was about six feet tall and in his late 20s. We left him a deposit and said we would be back in the late evening. I am not sure if he realized we were using his truck to move a plane since there was no need to give him these details. Carl drove to the barn that housed the plane. We unlocked the side door and entered the area to see what the move entailed. We needed to open the two sliding doors at the front of the barn, move the plane out to the truck, secure the plane to the truck, and then drive the truck with the plane attached to a hangar 30 miles away.

The first course of action was to open the barn's sliding doors to provide an exit point for the plane. The doors looked like they had not been used in 10 years. The doors were off the track, and vines had grown around all sides of the door. Since we had not anticipated this problem, we did not have the appropriate tools with us. Carl and I found some branches that we used to dig around the bottom of the door. We used the branches as levers to pry the door up onto the track after we had cleaned the track. These feats of strength were not easy for Carl and me. Both of us had office jobs and were not used to manual tasks. The doors were in place and now opened for the plane to exit. This was a two-passenger Cessna aircraft that had not been used for a while. The tires were flat; the plane could not be rolled anywhere. We looked around the barn for an air compressor. After a long search, we found it. Then we realized the electricity was turned off. That was the end of that avenue. Unfortunately, it was Sunday morning about 8 a.m., and there weren't many places open that could remedy the situation. Carl and I got in the truck and started to roam the neighborhood. Eventually, we did find an auto parts store open on Sunday. We bought a few cans of bottled air, which are used as a temporary fix for flat tires. We went back to the hangar and added the air to the tires easily.

The barn was a structure measuring 40 feet by 30 feet, separated in the center by three steel pillars. These pillars posed

Me as We (Relationships and Married Life)

a problem in moving the plane from the back of the hangar to the front opening, where the sliding doors were located. The main wings of the plane had previously been removed to fit into this barn, but the tail wings remained, measuring more than 15 feet across. We wondered how we could move the tail section past the steel pillars. Carl and I pushed the plane, now that the wheels were inflated, from the back of the hangar to the front, each time trying to get a better angle to go around the pillars and trying not to damage the tail section of the plane in the process. After 50 to 60 attempts, we managed to pass the pillars.

The area between where the truck was parked and the open barn doors was about 20 feet. Shrubs and small trees had made their home there since the plane first entered the barn. Carl and I used anything we could find in the barn to clear the path for the plane. This took about one hour. We could not clear the area well enough to move the plane through, so we backed the truck up to the barn-door opening. We put the back wheel of the plane in the bed of the truck, and this was enough to pull the plane to a clear area, where it could be more securely attached. We put a wooden box in the center of the rectangular truck bed. The plane's rear wheel was placed on the box and fastened to the four corners of the truck bed with a thick rope or hemp. If the plane swayed to any one side, we felt that the rope would hold the plane in the center of the truck bed.

It was now 2:30 p.m., and we were hoping to get the plane to the hangar before dark. With another four hours of daylight and only 30 miles to go, this seemed like a reasonable goal. Carl drove the truck. I was in the truck bed with the plane to make sure the ties did not come loose. The trip was slow but uneventful. Carl was driving the truck at a cautious 20 mph through the streets of Long Island. All was going as planned. Just as we were approaching a busy intersection, the traffic light turned red, and Carl had to stop the truck abruptly with the plane in tow. The truck stopped in time, but the plane didn't!

I was seated between the tail of the plane and the cab of the truck. The tail section was coming toward me, and I had about one second to duck. The tail went past me and smashed into the window of the cab, where Carl was sitting. There was broken glass all over Carl. The window was shattered, and the cab compartment was dented. Here we were, in the middle of a busy intersection, dragging a plane behind us that was no longer fastened to the truck, and Carl was covered in glass. The cost of having a moving company transport the plane seemed small compared to the possibility of having my head cut off, Carl being impaled with glass, and the valuable plane destroyed. This was turning out to be a lesson for future events — *if* we survived this one. With crowds of people gathering around, we managed to get the plane out of the intersection. We needed to re-tie the plane. How could we accomplish this and not have a reoccurrence at the next traffic light? Just then, a gentleman came out of the crowd, introduced himself as a stress engineer, and asked if we needed help. You bet we did. It was a miracle. How many stress engineers are there on the planet? Having one in the area see our dilemma and be willing to help was unbelievable! I could feel Carl's father looking down on us from above and doing his best to assist us in this challenge.

The plane was now securely fastened by the stress engineer. We proceeded through the towns of Long Island. As a child,

Me as We (Relationships and Married Life)

I would always visit my cousins in Smithtown. Never in my wildest dreams did I ever think I would be towing a plane through the small main road of that town. This is a two-lane road. Carl had to stay on the left part of our lane because the tail of the plane was just barely missing the telephone poles that lined the street. I never noticed those poles until we were driving a plane through the streets. Each pole brought out an instant sweat on both of us. Police cars were now behind us, signaling us to pull over. We made a right turn onto a wider road and stopped the truck. The police officer was astounded. He didn't know what to do. He said he'd never seen a plane come through the town. He looked in his manual to determine what type of ticket to give us, but this wasn't covered in the manual.

It was now 7:30 p.m., and the sun had already set. After radio conversations with the head of the police department, the officer gave us two choices. He could escort us past his town's line now, or we could park the truck and plane in the adjacent mall parking lot and wait until morning to continue. He assured us that, if we chose the latter, we would still be escorted. The policeman asked us to think it over and let him know our decision. Carl and I were both distraught and almost in tears. I say "almost" because we are grown-up males, who are not supposed to do those things. Should we take shifts eating and sleep in the cab that night in about 40-degree temperature? That wasn't too bad. But the idea of not finishing the trip today and extending our torture to another day was unthinkable. We decided to continue.

Three police cars were to escort us out of Smithtown and onto the Veterans Memorial Highway. We were told to follow them until we got onto the highway. We made it to the highway, but the police were still following us, and we wondered why. Again, we were pulled over, and the policeman explained that we had gotten onto the highway in the wrong direction. *Now what?* Much to our surprise, the police stopped the traffic on this major highway so that we could make a U-turn.

I couldn't believe we were finally laughing. The thought of us making a U-turn with a plane on the Veterans Memorial Highway with a police escort sent Carl and me into hysterics. What a story to tell our children.

At 11 p.m., we arrived at the hangar. What a relief. We opened the hangar doors and drove the plane in. We separated the plane from the truck. Using the headlights from the truck, we untied the rest of the plane and took the main wings out of the truck to leave in the hangar. Mission accomplished.

Only one problem remained: What would we tell the person we rented the truck from? How would we explain the damage that had been done? We didn't know him at all. Was he a violent person? Did he own guns? These were some of the thoughts that we discussed. We decided to leave the truck at a gas station about two blocks from his house, call him, and explain that there was some damage to the truck, that he should get an estimate, and that we would pay him for the repairs. We hoped this would be acceptable. I called and told him what had happened. He pleaded with me to bring the truck back. He said he could not leave the house since he was watching a neighbor's small children and couldn't leave them alone. We did not know if this was true or just a fabrication to get us there, so he could kill us for damaging his truck. We decided to bring the truck back.

Me as We (Relationships and Married Life)

However, Carl and I both had hammers in our hands when we approached his house. We didn't know what to expect, and I wasn't sure if we would actually use the hammers. Any adrenaline we had left was ready for action. He was waiting for us outside when we arrived at his house. To our surprise, he thanked us so much for returning his truck; the damage was almost unimportant.

We drove back to Carl's house, where his wife prepared us dinner. Just sitting down without trying to determine what challenge lay ahead was calming. I arrived home about 2 a.m. and told my wife what had transpired.

That was a day Carl and I would always remember.

Ten years after moving the plane, my daughter Daria was in college, and, as many college students do, she went to a psychic with her friends for fun. When it was Daria's turn, the psychic asked, "Was there someone in your family working on a plane?" Daria answered, "Yes." The psychic said, "He is still working on it." It had been 16 years since Savia's father had passed away and the plane was still at the museum in Bayport, where we left it. Later that month, Savia's brother Dario received a call from the people at the museum. They said that they had heard sounds coming from the locked hangar and lights would go on now and then at night. Dario took this as a sign that his father was still working on the plane from the other side and might need some help. He reactivated the project, assembled a world-class team, and is now fully engaged in having his father's invention to save lives come to fruition.

For more information: go to www.aviationsafety resources.com

Houseboat Hell
Rideau Lakes 1988

I did not realize that so much "stuff" would be needed to spend one week on a houseboat. Clothing for warm or cold weather, sun or rain, sleeping attire, dressy, casual, and less casual. This is just clothing we are talking about. Then there is food. Pots, pans, utensils, plates, glasses — all of this was only *some* of the "stuff" we were now loading onto the boat. After our eighth trip from the van to the boat, I wondered how all this started.

Savia and I were at a TFS convention in Bermuda. We were riding our motorbikes throughout the towns, admiring the beautiful landscapes and scenery, when I saw Phil and his wife, Julie, in the town of St. George. They had just gotten onto their bikes when they noticed me hollering "Follow us." I had seen Phil at business meetings but had not previously spoken to him for longer than two minutes. However, the atmosphere and timing seemed right for us to get better acquainted. Together, we rode through the streets of Bermuda, stopping now and then to take pictures and have lunch. We learned that they had two girls close to our children's ages. As time went on, we visited them at their home, and they at ours. The children seemed to become friends as quickly as we had become friends with Phil and Julie. We went on a barbecue together and really enjoyed ourselves.

Phil asked us if we would be interested in joining them on a houseboat they were to rent for a week at Rideau Lakes. The prospect of a weeklong boating trip on the lakes and canals during the summertime in Canada was very enticing. Phil said, "It's just like camping, only on water."

Me as We (Relationships and Married Life)

This trip would cost about $1,300 per family, which we were not prepared for. We told Phil that we would love to go on the trip with them; however, we would have to wait until next summer, about 18 months from then, to accumulate the funds for the trip. They agreed.

The day finally came. That morning in June of 1988, we had both driven about 250 miles with loaded vans and arrived at our departure point. There were four long wooden docks with about 20 houseboats in different stages of loading and unloading. It took eight of us about two hours to load the houseboat. We were surprised to see that our housemates had brought carpeting with them for the houseboat. These people were serious.

Once the boat was loaded, the instructor took us out for a navigational lesson. We took turns steering and learned how to start the boat, which side of the buoys to be on, upstream green on the left, downstream green on the right. Our entire course of instruction lasted 15 minutes. We were then supposedly ready to sail the seas.

As we started out, we were looking forward to a pleasant, relaxing week. Phil was the unofficial captain, since he had some boating experience. We had none. Our journey began by leaving the dock and heading out onto the Canadian lakes. Maneuvering this big house on the water was not easy. We managed to dock at our first town, tie the boat down, and walk around. The quaint shops and scenery were a beautiful sight. We left for the next town, where we encountered our first set of locks.

None of us had seen locks before. The way the locks worked was that the boats would go into part of the channel.

On the right side of the wall were cables. There was a pole with a hook on the end to grab onto the cable so that you could pull the boat against the wall. Once all the boats were secured, the doors in front of and behind you would close, and water would slowly be added to raise the level of water you were in, so that it was even with the next lock. What an interesting system of changing water levels. We didn't think it would be too difficult.

Use of a propane tank was not allowed at the locks. Since it was getting late, we thought it would be better if we ate before going through the locks. We anchored the boat about 300 yards from the lock and started our gas barbecue for dinner. It was very relaxing. We were sitting down eating, watching the currents in the water, when Phil started shouting out orders. "Bob and Julie — bring in the anchor. Savia — get to the steering wheel."

I didn't know what was going on, but I knew we had to leave — and fast. It seemed the boat had drifted into a row of rocks and was stuck on a cable. Phil accelerated the engine to full throttle, and we were able to crash through the rocks and head back toward the locks. After we were safely away, Phil explained why he'd acted that way. He said, "Do you remember seeing those ropes with the red flags?"

Yes, we did, but we didn't know what they were.

Well, Phil figured it out when he looked up and saw the scenery in a different location and heard the sound of running water. "Those flags meant that there was a waterfall nearby." We did not realize that our boat had drifted toward the waterfall. He contained his panicked state, so that we would not panic. It didn't really matter much that we broke the propeller going through the rocks. Now we knew what those red flags meant.

Me as We (Relationships and Married Life)

We drifted toward the waterfall because the anchor was not working properly. We read the manual that was in the boat and discovered that the rope the anchor was tied to was too short and would not stop us from drifting. This was more of a problem than we expected, because now, when we left one dock to arrive at the next, we were not sure if there was room for us to dock. If there wasn't, we had to anchor the boat — and now we knew that would not work. Each time we left a port, we wondered if there was space for us at the next dock.

As the days went by, the boat was becoming more difficult to handle. When we needed to make turns, it was not responding very well. It seemed that the electrical system in the boat was not working properly. *How could we tell?* you might ask. The boat would stall as we slowed down, and, at night, we noticed that only one light was dimly lit on the boat. The other lights were out.

We would all sit around the table at night, playing cards, with the one dim light over us. One evening, we were gathering our chairs together around the table when Phil left to find another chair. We were sitting around the table, ready to begin the card game, and expecting Phil to return any moment. We waited and waited, until finally, we decided he had been gone too long. I went to see what was taking so long. I couldn't believe my eyes. Even at night, I could see that someone had left the cover to the engine compartment open, and Phil had fallen in.

Using a flashlight, I could see that he was in pain. He was wedged into the space next to the engine. His foot was bent behind him, and his complexion was ghostly white. Together, we managed to bring him up from the compartment. Phil is not what you would call "small-framed," so this was not an easy feat. He was fortunate to suffer only fractured ribs. It could have been much worse. Although he was in pain for the remainder of the trip, he didn't let that interfere with his vacation.

It was wonderful to travel from port to port and see the towns along the waterway. As we traveled, we would stop, put down our anchor that didn't work, and sunbathe or water-bathe (swim). The boat had a water slide that the kids loved. Phil's two girls, Amy and Kari, and my daughter Tara couldn't get enough of the water slide. My daughter Daria, on the other hand, was sick with fever. Not only did she feel badly because she was sick, but, even more, she was tortured by the fact that she couldn't go into the water and use the slide. When would she get another chance at this experience? Perhaps never. Sometimes life is tough.

During the next day of travel, we came to even longer locks. Phil brought the boat into the first lock and tried to maneuver it close to the wall. I took the pole with the hook on the end to grab the cables that were on the side of the wall. This would allow us to keep the boat steady as the water level rose. The hook end of the pole grabbed the cable, and I pulled the pole toward me as hard as I could, since I was moving a large houseboat. The hook slipped off the cable, and the end of the pole hit me hard in the ribs. The pain was unexpected and severe. How many injured ribs does that make? This trip was not turning out to be as much fun as I was hoping for.

That night we docked at Smith Falls. During the day, we walked around the town, and the view of the locks and the falls was like a work of art. I remember thinking, *God really*

Me as We (Relationships and Married Life)

knew what he was doing when he created nature. At night, we heard some noise near the boat. We awoke to see two boys run away with our cooler, clothes-drying rack, and blanket. We didn't think that, in a place we thought of as paradise, there would be robbers. Fortunately, the items the boys stole were not essentials.

After several complaint calls, we returned to our initial point of departure to get new batteries. The boat did run a little better but not as well as we had hoped. Later, we found out that the new batteries had been connected on the opposite terminals. Therefore, turns and precise handling were still not possible.

It seemed that Julie liked cooking gourmet meals on the boat. She'd brought special silverware, place settings, wine glasses, cloth napkins, etc. This was not what Savia had expected to do on this trip. The thought of stopping at different ports and eating out every night was more like Savia had envisioned. Tension began to surface. When Savia was cleaning up after the gourmet meals, Julie began shouting, "Stop using the water. Don't you know our septic tank is almost full?" Savia had become somewhat disgusted over the living arrangements. Thank goodness there were only a few days left to our trip.

Julie's tone was startling, but her statement was correct. Our septic tank was full and needed to be pumped out, and we were also low on gasoline. We headed to the pumping station. Several hours later, we arrived. Our stomachs were unsettled when we saw the design of the pumping area. The docking area was about 150 yards from us. It was flanked on both sides by two rows of very expensive yachts. Our septic and gas tanks were at the back of the boat. This meant that we had to back the boat up 150 yards between the rows of yachts. There wasn't much room, and the electrical condition of our boat and our broken propellers made this an unpleasant experience. We slowly backed up the boat and were getting very close to some of the yachts. I guess the yacht owners could tell we were in trouble, because they were all hanging over their boats with the lock poles in their hands ready to help us and stop us from damaging their boats. Very slowly, we managed to empty the septic tank and refill the gas tank. The stress was too much. We needed a vacation from our vacation.

After an exciting and torturous week, we were docked and unloading the boat. We were checking out at the office and hoping to get our deposit back, but we weren't sure how the broken propellers would be handled. We were asked to pay for the propellers. We explained that, because the electrical system and anchor did not work properly — and our training consisted of only 15 minutes — Phil had fractured two ribs, and we had almost gone over a waterfall. They would just have to absorb the cost of replacing the broken propeller. They agreed.

They also gave us coupons, so that if we wanted to return, the second couple would be at no charge. Do you think we took advantage of this great offer? *Absolutely not!!!!!!!*

As we were driving back home, we noticed that it took 15 minutes by car to pass the same towns along the waterway that it took us one week to see by boat.

Even though the trip had been a disaster, it left us with an unbelievable experience and memories. It was like the Army. I am glad I did it, but I wouldn't want to do it again.

Me as We (Relationships and Married Life)

The Eye Venture
Mom's Eyes

In 1990, Mom was diagnosed with macular degeneration, a serious eye disease that causes blindness. Although this is not hereditary, two of her sisters and her brother had the same problem. Her eye doctor referred her to whom he thought was the best specialist to handle her worsening vision. I accompanied Mom and Dad to the doctor in the Bronx. After a thorough exam, the doctor recommended eye surgery. I asked, "How many previous operations like this have you performed?" He said "20." Then I asked, "How many were successful"? This seemed to stump him. "What do you mean by 'successful'?" he said. My response was "How many patients could see better following the operation?" He replied, "None." I said, "So, instead of Mom going blind slowly, you want it to be immediate? No, thanks," and we left.

I contacted Dr. Kelly, who had been a great resource for us throughout the years. He recommended a former ophthalmologist, Dr. Beigelson, who now practiced in Arizona, using non-conventional methods. Three days later, Mom, Dad, and I were on a plane to Mesa, Arizona. When we first met the doctor, we were a little shocked by his appearance. He was about 50 years old, tall, thin, looking like Cyrano de Bergerac, and he had a long ponytail draping down his back. We wondered what we had gotten ourselves into, but a recommendation from Dr. Kelly could not be taken lightly. We proceeded. He tested her to determine which remedies would work best and then injected these remedies down the front of her chest, into her stomach, below her eyes, and into her forehead. She was amazingly brave, while Dad and I cringed without Mom noticing. We were there for a week while Mom underwent treatments.

During the non-treatment days, we explored Arizona. On one excursion, we got out of the car to look at the scenery. Dad was walking on the edge of a 300-foot cliff, and I had to object. His fearlessness was making me too nervous. Perhaps he was just observing and didn't actually want to fall off. From then on, he was not allowed out of the car when heights were involved. The doctor sent us home with Conisan B, a natural eye remedy, which Mom continued to take. When this was not available, a client of mine who visited Germany for business would bring some back. This stopped the progression of the disease for 15 years. Much better than no-success eye surgery.

Talk About Risk!
Is This Our Dream House?

Savia and I had been living at Sanford Drive for 12 years, and things had changed from the time that we'd purchased the house. We now had two children, our income had improved to $80,000 a year, new-home developments were sprouting up everywhere, and the home we'd purchased for $43,000 was now worth $180,000. In our town of Randolph alone, there were 20 new developments being constructed. We thought it was time for a move.

We were very interested in a home in Chester. The asking price was $373,000. Although the house was beautiful from the outside, the layout didn't make sense. The front door and side door should have been reversed. Was it even possible to go from an $180,000 home to a $373,000 home? The real estate agent said that, if we didn't buy the home today, the price would increase tomorrow. Great sales tactic, but it

Me as We (Relationships and Married Life)

didn't work. We felt that the financial burden would be too much and kept looking. By June 1989, we had deposits on two houses, Burnet Brook and Cromwell Crossing, and on a piece of land simultaneously. We were really serious about a move. The dream of a new home was getting closer.

As Savia and I were driving around our area, we saw a trailer on the side of South Road that looked like the beginning of a construction site. That was enough to pique our interest. Savia went into the trailer and met Gerry Novak. He was the builder and architect who was putting together yet another development. However, this one was a little different. On a 100-year-old apple orchard, there was a 50-acre man-made lake where 25 custom homes would be built on one side and another 25 on the other side. But this development was still in the planning stages. We could not see the lake, and the trees had just been cleared for a dirt path. If you were going to build a home from scratch, what would it look like? What style would it be? During our travels, we had seen a home on Roxiticus Road in Mendham that really caught our attention. It was a 15,000-square-foot "Country French"-style home. WOW!! Could we build something like that? It just so happened that this home was on the market. We visited four or five times while there was an open house, under the pretense of seriously considering buying the house. We were even able to obtain the house plans.

We brought these plans to Gerry Novak and asked if he could give us an estimate for a scaled-down version of the Mendham house. He came back with a 4,300-square-foot version with a completely redesigned interior for $605,000. *Since the $373,000 house in Chester was too expensive, we decided to have the $605,000 house built.* Some decisions defy reason.

All the building lots were available except one. The Packins were the first to have a house built. We could not afford a house on the lake or the one we were buying either. Our criteria for the lot were a level backyard and a high lot, since we didn't want water problems; the kitchen and family room had to face south, since that is where we are most of the time; there had to be no sidewalks to shovel and no water hydrant in the front. The result was **5 Canterbury Court,** the highest lot in the development. The contract was signed, and we were on our way.

The new house was only about two miles from the old house. So, every evening on my way home from a client appointment, I would stop by the new house to see the progress. It was several months before construction started, but

Me as We (Relationships and Married Life)

that didn't stop me from passing by every day to see the dirt and dream.

As construction started, we needed to make decisions about cabinets, floors, colors, etc. Each decision was compared to the initial estimate and was either a debit or credit from the original price. After all the adjustment, the house price was now $645,000. How could we afford this? *We couldn't.* Our contract stated that, once we received the certificate of occupancy, we had 30 days for the house closing to take place, or the penalty would be $150 per day. We were busy choosing appliances, cabinets, roofing, etc., with the growing concern that we were making these choices for someone else. We would often drive down South Road singing, "Didn't We Almost Have It All?" by Whitney Houston.

Our Sanford Drive house was on the market but not selling. Could we buy a house we couldn't afford and pay the mortgage and expenses on the Sanford Drive house? No chance.

We applied for a No-Income-Verification Loan, stating our income to be $250,000. This would allow us to borrow almost the amount we needed to close on the house. The $40,000 worth of upgrades could not be added to the mortgage. So, we were $40,000 short. We still had Sanford Drive to pay.

The $150-per-day penalty had been in progress for about a month. Along with the builder, we also wanted to close on the house. However, the penalty cost less than our mortgage. When we told the builder, he said he didn't realize the penalty should have been higher.

The builder was eager to sell the house, but we didn't have the additional $40,000.

It would be very difficult for him to sell a house that had been custom made for us to anyone else in a reasonable time period. We asked for a $40,000 loan from the builder to help us close the deal. He agreed to a two-year loan.

As insane as it now seems, our plan was to use the $40,000 to help us make mortgage payments and give me two years time to dramatically improve my income and sell Sanford Drive.

Somehow, we got through it. Five years in the house had gone by, and my mother would call and say "I still hear the echoes. I guess you don't have furniture yet." After hanging in there for five years, we thought it was time to wallpaper the kitchen. Savia had seen a model home in Chester that was beautifully decorated. She called the interior decorator, Joanne Wilker.

We told her we wanted to wallpaper the kitchen. She said she was coming with some of her associates. She came with carpenters, flooring people, curtain people, and painters. They took pictures, made copies of our house plans, and measured everything.

During our next appointment with Joanne, not only did she have three examples of possible wallpaper candidates but an overall plan for how our house would ultimately look. The fabrics, colors, and furnishings were like a *Better Homes and Gardens* centerfold. Even though the wallpaper was the only improvement we could make, the idea of progress toward the dream décor captured our imagination. I would never go to anyone else for house decorating. Joanne held the dream. This also applied to financial planning. I would not give someone just an IRA but would design an entire plan. In August 1994, Savia's mom passed away, leaving us an inheritance. This helped with decorating and college for Daria and Tara. As of September 2010, we were in our house 20 years, and all decorating had been completed, except for the master bedroom, which was never painted. I guess it was time.

Part of History
Garth Brooks Concert

My daughter Tara is a big Country Music fan, and after hearing several songs, Savia and I became fans, too. We were so enamored with Garth Brooks' songs that we listened to his CDs while we drove through the Italian countryside on vacation. So, when Tara found out there was a free concert in Central Park on Thursday, August 7, 1997, she asked if we wanted to go. We had never attended any concerts in the past and liked Garth Brooks, so we decided to take the day off from work and accompany Daria, Tara, and her friend Jud. With a free concert in Central Park, we knew there would be a crowd — a big crowd — so we wanted to get there early to get close to the stage. The concert was scheduled to start at 8 p.m.

After eating breakfast and packing our lunch and snacks, we left our house at 4:30 a.m. for the concert. As we were driving in, we realized that we needed blankets to sit on to reserve our space. Should we go back home and arrive later for the concert? We'd rightfully equated our arrival time with our distance from the stage, and therefore, we didn't want to stop. However, the blankets were a required accessory. Because the stores were closed at that time in the morning, we were not sure where to obtain blankets. Savia thought of stopping at a hotel to ask if we could borrow two blankets. Fortunately, the hotel was accommodating and agreed to give us the blankets, and then we continued on our way. We parked our car and arrived at the park around 6 a.m. The entrance to the park was closed. There was no choice but to wait, and, since there were not many people ahead of us, everything looked like it was going great. About 7:50 a.m., we realized that we were not as fortunate as we had thought. There were other entrances to the park, and those entrances were being opened before ours. When our entrance opened, we got as close to the stage as we could, about 300 feet back. We opened our blankets and staked out our spot. This is where we would be for the next 12 hours. The park was well organized, with food stands and bathrooms a reasonable distance from everyone.

There was not an inch of grass untouched by a blanket. This was not the rebellious, Woodstock-type crowd. This was a country music crowd. When someone passed your blanket for food or a restroom break, they took off their shoes and walked on the blanket's perimeter. These people were polite, respectful, and well-mannered. How refreshing. It was a perfect summer day, with a clear, blue sky, not too hot, low humidity, and friendly people. Time went by quickly, and we were all ready for the show to begin.

Garth came out on schedule at 8 p.m. and really knew how to work up the crowd. Everyone was standing during the entire concert. All the songs I had heard from Tara's albums were there live. Have you ever seen the inside of a speaker — the woofers and tweeters that actually vibrate to produce the sound? We were standing about 100 feet from these monstrous speakers, and our bodies were vibrating to the music and acting as the woofers and tweeters. I could feel my heart beating to the rhythm of the music, which was a little uncomfortable. During the concert, Garth said that, when he'd scheduled his performance in Central Park in

Me as We (Relationships and Married Life)

Manhattan, he did not know if many people would show up. After all, are New Yorkers fans of country music? Billy Joel and Don McLean were guest musicians to add to the excitement. In the middle of "Unanswered Prayers," Garth stopped singing, and the crowd of New Yorkers sang his lines. Yes, we were fans and knew all the words. What greater honor can be bestowed upon a musician? Being in the middle of the crowd singing and dancing, with the speakers sending sound waves through my body was the closest I have ever been to a religious, trance-like experience.

When the concert was over, everyone headed out. There was a four-foot rock wall with an opening through which we were expected to exit. However, the mass of people leaving made the waiting line unrealistic, so we decided to help each other climb over the wall. It felt like *Escape from Alcatraz*.

So, now, we were part of history. We were part of the almost 1 million people who showed up, the biggest crowd ever in Central Park.

Attitude Is Everything
Joey's Baseball Game

My cousin John's son, Joey, was in the Baseball State Championship Playoffs in a town close to my home. I told John I would be there to see him play. Savia, the kids, and I got into our new Ford Expedition SUV, purchased just the week before. It was a large, monster-size car that we thought we needed for the snowy, icy winters we were having. We arrived at the ballpark early, parked the car, and walked to see Joey and his team. As I was sitting there in the spectator seats, I realized that my new car was parked just over the outfield fence, an excellent target for a home run. I decided to move the car farther back in the parking lot, away from the outfield fence. It was the third inning, and the game was close. The opposing team had runners on first and second with one out.

The next batter hit a long home run over the fence, passing most cars and landing on my windshield.

You could hear the sound of everyone in unison, "Ow," when the ball crushed the glass. John and I went to survey the damage. I thought car windshields could not shatter. I was wrong. There were little pieces of glass everywhere. We got as much of the glass into a bag as we could. John was upset, as most people would be, about the damage to my car. I sort of accepted that the damage had been done and that there was nothing I could do about it. We walked back to see the remainder of the game. I noticed the player who had hit the home run sitting in the dugout. There was a fence between him and me. I walked up to the dugout and said in a moderately angry tone, "Hey, number 27 — you just smashed the windshield of my new car." There was a long pause while he waited for my next words. I continued, "That was a tremendous home run! I didn't think you could hit it that far. Congratulations — that is what you are supposed to do." He smiled and responded with a sheepish "Thank you." When the game was over, we brushed some more glass fragments off the seats, laid down some towels, and drove home.

> "It is not what happens to you, but how you react that makes the difference."
> — *Robert Giarraffa*

> "Attitude Is Everything."
> — *Jim Rohn*

Me as We (Relationships and Married Life)

From Physical to Spiritual
Alabama Trip — November 20 to December 7, 2015

Savia was having some health-related issues and was operated on to resolve the problem. This turned out to be only a partial solution. We were looking for additional steps we could take to improve her situation. One of our trusted doctors, Dr. Lynne August, told us about a treatment in Alabama that could help. It was modeled after the groundbreaking work of Royal Rife, known for his Rife Machine, in the 1930s. Although he had remarkable success with his device, it was difficult for anyone to duplicate, since he was not a great record keeper. Was it worth a shot? We thought so.

So, on November 20, 2015, Savia and I piggy-backed a family trip to Disney with a health trip to Pelham, Alabama. We met the manufacturer of the recreated Rife Machine and toured his electronic-devices company. Before our trip, we were aware that the device was not yet in production. However, the treatment was available at the owner's home, and since it took 1½ hours every other day, we had plenty of free time.

We had not been to this part of the country before and did not know what to expect. We went out to breakfast and noticed that many families and couples were inconspicuously bowing their heads and saying a prayer before they began to eat. It appeared to us that they were not doing this to get attention or show that they were religious. It was different from up north. And although Birmingham was well known in the '60s for racial discrimination, it seemed to be absent today. Everyone was a college football fan and were discussing the teams, upcoming games, and rivalries at length. While we were at the hotel, we met several men in construction who were there, away from home for months at a time, working on a job site. They were doing whatever it took to provide for their family. Overall, it looked like a great place to live. It felt like America as it should be.

We asked at the front desk of our hotel if there were any sightseeing places to visit. The girl said that she had been to this place about an hour away that had miniature reproductions of some of the famous historical buildings — she said we had to see it. Why not?

We were in Alabama with nothing else to do, so we went for a drive. On the way there, we passed a beautiful church that had two steeples. I hadn't seen that before and thought that, if we had enough time on the way back, we would stop there for a closer look. The miniature buildings turned out

Me as We (Relationships and Married Life)

to be the "Ave Maria Grotto," the lifetime work of Brother Joseph Zoettl, a Benedictine monk of St. Bernard Abbey. With stone, concrete, and anything else he could find around the grounds, he replicated 125 world-famous buildings in great detail, including The Colosseum, St. Peter's Church in Rome, The Mission at Santa Barbara in California, and the Grotto at Fatima. One building would have taken me a lifetime, but I guess he lived to a very old age.

On our way back to the hotel, we did stop at that church with the two steeples. It was the Sacred Heart of Jesus Catholic Church. We got out of our car to take a picture of the church when a truck pulled up alongside of us. A man got out of the truck, walked up to us, introduced himself as the pastor, and asked if he could help us. We told him we were admiring the structure. He asked if we wanted our picture taken together

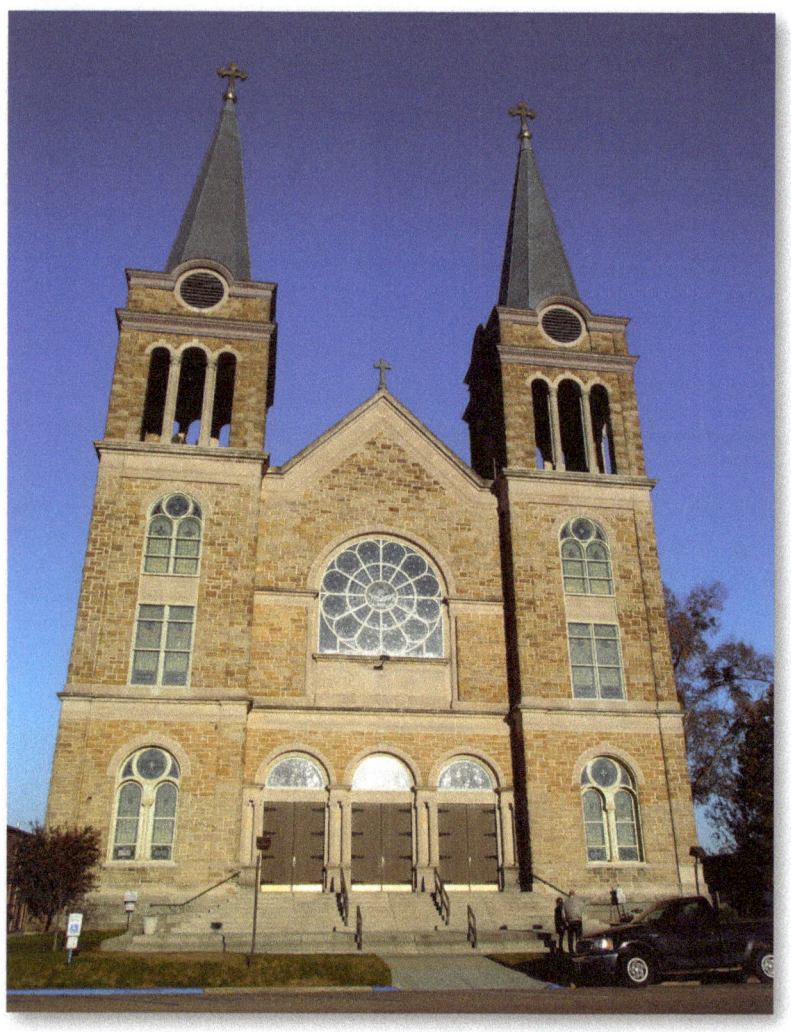

with the church in the background and if we wanted a tour of the inside. We agreed to both.

On the way out of the church, the pastor asked if we had been to The Shrine of the Most Blessed Sacrament. He said

Me as We (Relationships and Married Life)

that as long as we were here in Alabama and were this close, we should stop there to see the grounds.

The next morning, after Savia's treatment, we added this to our agenda for the day. It was about a 90 minute ride to the shrine in Hanceville. The driveway to the shrine seemed about 10 miles long and opened up to a peaceful grouping of buildings situated on a 400-acre site and a religious center affiliated with the Eternal Word Television Network (EWTN), founded by Mother Angelica, a Catholic nun like no other. She single-handedly brought a religious station to TV with no funds. Was it a coincidence that we happened to be in this particular section of Alabama? I don't believe in coincidences (read *The Celestine Prophecy*). You could feel the sanctity and heavenly presence on the grounds.

Speaking with some of the other people at the Shrine, they mentioned that they also visited Caritas of Birmingham. A few days later, after Savia's treatment, we went to Caritas.

Caritas of Birmingham is a mission located about 20 miles southeast of Birmingham, Alabama. It is a community that lives at the mission and celebrates apparitions of The Virgin Mary, similar to Mary's visit in Medjugorje. More than 150 apparitions have taken place at this location.

It seemed as if we were being guided in each step of our journey — The Grotto, the two-steeple church, The Shrine, and Caritas. Our *physical*-healing trip was transforming into a *spiritual*-healing trip.

We decided to attend mass on Sunday at the closest Catholic church. There were gorgeous flowers on the altar. After mass, Savia asked me to get the camera out of the car to take some pictures of the beautifully decorated altar. She said she would sit and pray awhile.

When I returned, Savia told me that, while I was away, and people were leaving the church after the mass, something interesting happened. Out of the corner of her eye, she saw an elderly woman, dressed in vibrant purple. She came up to Savia and whispered in her ear, "Don't worry — everything will be alright." Savia said that when she turned around, the woman was gone. Of course, Savia's first reaction was to be annoyed. *Who was this woman? Did I look like I was sick? What nerve!*

As she got into the car to leave, Savia thought about her experience. She was so upset with herself for not being more accepting. "This woman looked a little out of place — and how could she know what I was thinking? Could it have been an angel?" That was her conclusion.

As I said, our trip turned into a guided spiritual journey, culminating in a visit from an angel. A miracle did take place — and Savia has been fine ever since.

A Kid Again
Grandmasters Softball

I played stickball and stoop ball growing up on the streets of Brooklyn but not on an actual ballfield, with dirt, grass, and real bases. I waited until age 50 to be in my first official ball game. The "softball" was harder than the rubber ball of the old days. I answered an ad in the local newspaper for a team that was looking for players. The team had no sponsor, so I volunteered New Horizons to sponsor the team. I played second base, shortstop, and right field and was having a ball. Pun intended. There was an informal tally of the wins and losses of each team but no player statistics. What is baseball without statistics? Being a "documenter," I started keeping track of wins and losses for each team and emailing the standings to the managers. Next was an Excel spreadsheet that tracked each New Horizons player's statistics. Each week, the game statistics were sent to each player with YTD summary. The All-Time Top 10 Leaders in each category was published at year's end. This gave the players something to shoot for and helped with motivation. For about 10 years, I held the record for most consecutive hits — eight — until Mario, the manager, who had been playing almost professionally since he was 15, shattered my record with 15 consecutive hits. Now that's hitting! In 2008, our team won the championship, and parties ensued.

A Blessed and Guided Life

Grandmasters kick off their new softball season

RANDOLPH TWP. — The Randolph/Roxbury Grandmasters over 48 mens softball league kicked off their sixth season on April 30 with a total of 62 runs scored in the first two games.

Opening day jitters and rusty fielding combined with strong, gusty winds blowing toward the outfield helped Cheli's Diehards and New Horizon Financial start the year with victories. The Diehards went up 7-0 against the Over-the-Hill Gang in the first inning. Later, the Gang came back to go ahead 9-8 but couldn't hold the lead.

The Diehards, powered by homers from Bob Banghart and Kim Becker, were way too much as the Gang lost 21-11.

The second game also was a slugfest with New Horizon Financial edging out a 16-15 win over last season's champs, Another World Travel.

Another World Travel got plenty of hitting from the middle of their lineup, with Jamie Lubin, Bob Laurie and Howie Stien accounting for 12 hits and 10 runs. But New Horizon had six big, power hitters knocking the ball off the outfield fences for doubles and triples and were led by rookie left fielder, Phil Garber.

The game ended with the go ahead run at the plate hitting a smash to deep right field that was tracked down, bobbled but held on to, by Bob Giaraffa for the final out.

Two new teams from Roxbury will join the league next week. The standings as of May 1 are: Cheli's Diehards 1-0, New Horizon Fincancial Services 1-0, Another World Travel 0-1, Over-the-Hill Gang 0-1, Roxbury Blue 0-0 and Roxbury Gold 0-0.

Me as We (Relationships and Married Life)

Around 2009, I broke my ankle in pre-season practice. After that, I played only when there were not enough players (which was most of the time). By 2017, many of our players who had been together for the past 20 years were now competing with much younger players. As a result, during our 15-game seasons of 2016 and 2017, we had only one win. We did an excellent job of recruiting before the start of the 2018 season and brought our team back from the dead. I called us the Lazarus Team. The weather for the 2018 season was very unusual. Our three pre-season practices were canceled due to frozen snowy fields, and the rain canceled four other games. On May 13, Mother's Day, the weather forecast was rain all day. At 8 a.m., it was raining, and John, the commissioner, said that the 9 a.m. game was on. I don't know how he knew or who he prayed to, but the rain stopped. We were winning 8 to 7, and the opposing team was up in the bottom of the

New Horizons Softball Team 2015

ninth. The first three batters hit singles to load the bases with nobody out. Our chances for success looked grim. Then something extraordinary happened. Their batter hit a ground ball to our shortstop Dennis, who tagged the runner going to third base, threw the ball to Jeff, our second baseman, for the second out, and Jeff threw the ball to Dave at first base for a game-ending, walk-off triple play. Our team was jumping up and down, screaming and shouting like little kids, and I was thrilled to be a part of it. I thought this was a rare occurrence, so I looked up how many perfect games were pitched in all of baseball history as a comparison. The answer is 23. A walk-off Triple Play is even more rare with only nine. The game ended at 10:30 a.m., and the rain started again.

The next day, we all went back to our regular lives. But our lives were no longer regular. We had become part of history. This would be told to our children and grandchildren. Am I overdoing it? I don't think so.

The Move of a Lifetime
Mom at 92

Part I – The Roof

As I left my mother's house in Brooklyn, a roof shingle resting in the front yard was the only indication that hurricane Sandy had visited. The house where I grew up with my cousins, aunts, and uncle was now home to Mom and tenant Sally. At age 92, it was the only home Mom had ever known.

About every two weeks, I would visit Mom and now looking up, I could see some inconsistent areas where shingles were missing. I called Tom, our roofer, whom we had been working with for the past 10 years whenever repairs were

Me as We (Relationships and Married Life)

needed. He seemed to know what he was doing and charged a fair price as far as I could tell. I discussed the roof situation with my cousin Rose, who was a one-half owner, and my sister Loretta, who was a one-quarter owner, as was I. Rose wondered if the homeowner's insurance policy we had would cover the repairs. Although Hurricane Sandy had passed through New York and New Jersey, leaving a trail of devastation in its path, our house in Brooklyn was mostly spared, except for damage to the roof.

Travelers Insurance said they would send someone out to inspect the roof. After the inspection, they said the entire removal of the shingled roof and the new replacement roof would be covered but not the flat roof. That sounded like "an offer we could not refuse." I asked Tom, the roofer, to give me an estimate to replace the entire roof that I could submit to the insurance company who would be making the payments. A month later, I heard from Tom. It seems that he handled only repairs and that this job was too big for him. However, he did have a friend with a roofing company who could handle this for me for $14,000. I said "Great. Send me a written proposal." Another month went by, and then two more months. I continued calling Tom. I never heard from Tom again. I needed to find another roofing company.

Mom's friend Agnes said that several roofers advertised in the church bulletin. I called every one of them, with no response. I heard that a neighbor down the street was a contractor who did roofs. After many attempts, I finally got to speak with him. He was very busy with 22 homes he was constructing but said that he would get back to me. As you might expect, that never happened, even after several additional calls.

Mom's house has what is called an "attached house." It shared a roof with the house next to Mom's. Since the owner of the attached house was a builder, I asked him if he would consider the roofing job. He said that he would get back to me with an estimate. That never happened, either.

I was starting to get a little nervous. Nine months had passed since the insurance company's generous offer. I called them to ask how long I had to make the repairs. "Two years" was the answer. My cousin Vinny, Rose's husband, an architect, after hearing about my failed attempts to have the roof fixed, asked if he could help. He said Home Depot and Lowe's did roofs. Why hadn't I thought of that? What a simple solution. He called me the next week with the news. Both of these companies do roofs — but not half roofs. Their work could not be guaranteed if an adjoining roof was involved.

More than a little frustrated, I called Travelers and asked if they knew any roofing companies they could refer us to. They found eight of them. I called each of them and discovered that only one, Branch Restoration, would work in Brooklyn. They were willing to do the work for our adjoining roof and provide a written estimate and guarantee. I'd hit the jackpot.

I was now dealing with another "Tom," — Tom O'Keefe, from Branch Restoration. On **October 8, 2013,** I sent in my 30% deposit of $2,814 and was told that the work should start in four to six weeks. After four weeks had passed, I called for a time estimate, and I continued to call once every week after that. It seemed they were not finished with their previous job, it had snowed, it had rained, it was too cold, and, best of all, their roofer had quit. Tom sounded sincere when he said that was OK, since he had a new roofer starting next month, and he did not want to lose the job. What was my other option?

Me as We (Relationships and Married Life)

As far as I knew, none. So, I waited. The roof was started the beginning of April 2014, seven months after they'd received the deposit. But at least it was done. Tom was waiting for the payment. The contractor who owned the adjoining house, whom I had asked for an estimate, redid the roof on his half of the house. Why he never got back to me still remains a mystery.

On a visit to see Mom, I noticed that the roof looked different from the other roofs in the area. There was a gap between the wall and the roof shingles. I sent pictures to my cousin Vinny, who said they'd forgotten to add the flashing. This was serious. What type of roofer forgets to add flashing, and what was the quality of the job he'd performed? This confirmed my need for a warranty. Tom had the roofer install the flashing, and on May 15, I asked him for the bill. On May 24, Sally, the upstairs tenant, said there was a ceiling leak in her apartment and that she'd put down pots to collect the water. I emailed Tom, the insurance company, and the co-owners, making them aware of the leaking roof. Two weeks later, on June 10, when I spoke to Tom, he said that his roofer was looking into correcting the problem but didn't know if he'd completed the work or not but would get back to me.

I called and emailed Tom several times, with no response. On **October 2, 2014,** I told his secretary, Amanda, that if I received the warranty, I would send payment for the balance of the bill, about $12,000. On October 16, I called Amanda again, asking for the warranty and hoping to pay my outstanding bill. She said she was aware that I needed the warranty and was in the process of preparing it.

When my cousin Vinny went to Brooklyn to view the finished roof job, he noticed that the structural beam connecting the front porch and the roof looked uneven. Being an architect, this made him suspicious of a possible structural problem with this beam. He suggested that we unofficially have an engineer look at the house and give us his assessment. Were we willing to pay someone $2,500 to examine the house and give us an intelligent evaluation of its condition? After a long conference call with Savia and me, Rose, Vinny, and my sister Loretta in Arizona, we decided to hire the engineer. Vinny walked through the house with the engineer, and a week later, August 12, we received the inspection report. The back steps from my mother's kitchen to the backyard had no support. The concrete-and-stone pillars were decayed. The beam above the porch, which partially supported the second floor, ran around the entire length of the wraparound porch and was definitely compromised, but to what degree was uncertain, since it had a material covering it that we did not want to disturb. Now that we were aware of the poor condition of the house, what should we do?

Part 2 — The Move

My father and uncle had bought the house at 2328 83rd St. in Bensonhurst, Brooklyn, in 1954. Mom and Dad lived on the first floor with me and my sister Loretta. Mom's sister, Aunt Rose, and Uncle Ralph lived on the second floor with their daughter, Rose (we called her "Posey"), who was seven years older than me. Aunt Jo, another of Mom's sisters, lived on the third floor with her two sons, John and Bernie. Over the years, the porch had been remodeled twice, from old wood to beautiful wood and marbleized columns to brick. It was a wraparound porch like no other in the neighborhood. Many days, we would sit on the porch and talk. Neighbors would

Me as We (Relationships and Married Life)

stop by to chat. Passersby would always smile and say "Hello" on their way past.

There was a string of women who came from 10 a.m. to 5 p.m. on the weekdays to provide care for Mom. Two of them died. One broke her ankle on icy steps at her home, one had blood cancer, and one was just outright lazy. At 92, Mom was outlasting all of them. When the aide wasn't there, we would call the upstairs tenant, Sally, and ask if she could look in on Mom. She would make breakfast, lunch, or dinner as needed. Mom's 10 prescription drugs were a nightmare. She could not remember if she had taken them, so we needed to make other arrangements. The aides took care of this, but, with the ever-changing parade of people and the unpredictable schedule, was Mom taking the medicine as prescribed or taking them twice? What if she ran out of medicines? Who would know and reorder them? Some aides would handle that properly, I think, and others, not so much. We would find out on Wednesday that the aide had not been there on Monday or Tuesday. These aides charged only half the price of an agency aide, but there were obvious disadvantages.

We, as owners, discussed what to do with the house and Mom. With the structural integrity of the house in question, was it possible that it could last another 10 years without major repairs? Maybe. Was it also possible that, with the next winter storm, the weight of the snow on the roof could collapse the beam supporting the second floor? That was also a possibility. How would we feel if Mom or Sally were injured or worse, not to mention the lost value on the house? Mom always said, "When I am gone, you could sell this house for a lot because of the great porch." I told her I would sell the house but never the porch — it meant too much to her.

A Blessed and Guided Life

After a very long conference call among the owners and their spouses, we decided that the best course of action was to sell the house and eliminate the chance of the roof collapsing, with its obviously horrible consequences. Automatically, the next question that came up was, "What do we do with Mom and Sally, the tenant?"

At this stage in life, Mom did not even leave the house — no shopping, no church around the corner, no visiting neighbors. The house was her world. My sister Loretta in Arizona had suggested for years that Mom move there, since she loved the heat and did not like being alone in winter, when porch-sitting may not have been possible. Our options were assisted living near our house in New Jersey, living with us in our house, or living with Loretta in her house. We eliminated assisted living in New Jersey because we wanted her to be with her family and the cost was prohibitive. Mom was not able to handle the steps in my house, so Loretta's ranch style house seemed to fit her needs. Loretta said that arrangement was fine with her, since Mom had taken care of us for many years, and Savia and I took care of Mom for many years, and now it was her turn. We agreed that Mom should live with Loretta, but we had no idea how to get her there!

A little background on my sister Loretta's situation: Her husband, Frank, had passed away on the way to work at age 42, leaving Loretta with two young children — a difficult situation to be in. Loretta went to work. Because she was bored easily, she changed jobs about every two years, although she had stayed at the last place, Voya, for 11 years. When she left the jobs, she did not leave her friends — she collected them. Her daughter, Andrea, had always wanted to move to Arizona. She said it was the only state she knew of without

Me as We (Relationships and Married Life)

any natural disasters. So, at age 21, she moved to Arizona to start her adult life. Two years later, Loretta followed and loved the desert heat and the many activities available to her, including volunteering for everything. Now that Loretta is retired, she and Andrea have a catering company, L&D Eats, LLC, together, and they take only the jobs that come by word of mouth. Loretta teaches cooking classes once a month in the winter months and plans to start dinners for 25 people on her 800-square-foot patio in October 2019. Cooking is her passion, and baking is Andrea's. They work well together.

Loretta's son, Steven, is a New Jersey real estate developer, in the style of Donald Trump. There is nothing he can't accomplish.

Back to the house. After everyone in the house had passed away, Mom was in the house by herself. We were looking for a tenant and some companionship for Mom. Mom's friend, neighbor, and aide at the time, Mary, suggested a longtime friend, Sally, as a possible tenant. The place Sally was renting was being sold, and she was looking to move. Sally was 82 years old, about 4 foot 8 inches short, with a complexion and walk of someone around 70, and a roommate, Joe, a friendly guy about 84 years old. Sally had known Mom and her sisters for many years from church activities and church trips Mom's friend Agnes would run.

In July 2006, Sally and Joe moved into the second and third floors, where Aunt Rose, Uncle Ralph, and Aunt Jo had lived. The porch was a great meeting place for Mom, Sally, Joe, and many neighbors and friends who wanted to join them. As time went on, Joe became seriously ill and passed away. Sally got a dog to keep her company. He was a cute little dachshund who would come running to Mom while she was sitting on the porch and jump on her lap. Sally asked if it was OK to have the dog. I asked if it was housebroken and then said "OK." About a year later, Sally's stepdaughter lost her job and was wondering if she and her daughter could stay with Sally temporarily until she found employment.

Questions remained. How do we move Mom to Arizona? How do we handle Sally, the tenant? And when should the house be sold? We all reluctantly decided that the house should be sold before the first big snowstorm to someone who would take the house "as is" and be willing to make major renovations. It was now August 12, meaning we had to move fast. We needed some strategy for having prospective buyers see the house without making Mom aware that the house was to be sold.

On **August 14, 2014,** Sally called me and said that, while she and Mom were sitting on the porch, several people stopped to ask about the sale of the house. I told her I didn't know what she was talking about and that the house was not for sale. When I relayed this strange occurrence to my cousin Vinny, he added some perspective. He said that he'd gone to Zillow.com to see if he could find out what the house was worth and may have inadvertently put the house up for sale. He came to this realization because he was receiving calls from prospective buyers. Now, what do we do? We did want to sell the house but not until we gave Sally time to leave and somehow moved Mom to Arizona.

Vinny handled the negotiations with prospective buyers. At that time, that section of Brooklyn was in demand, especially by Chinese people. Several people came with bags of cash; another said he was representing his parents and would pay us $50,000 more than our asking price, if we gave him back the $50,000 after the sale. We were not ready for this type of

Me as We (Relationships and Married Life)

negotiation. Another couple was very interested in the house, even though they had not yet seen the inside.

The plan was to have Mom visit my daughter Daria, a 45-minute car ride, for the day while Vinny and Rose showed the house. It was not easy, but we did manage to drive Mom to Daria's house. She loved it and played with her grandchildren most of the time. It was a wonderful day for her.

The couple liked the house so much that that day they offered to buy our house at the asking price, however they needed to have the house closing by October 15th. That meant we had two months to move Sally and Mom out.

We told Sally the house was to be sold but not to tell my Mom, since it would upset her. She agreed. We told Sally we would help her with the moving expenses, but since Sally was a "hoarder," this would not be an easy move.

This is when past, long-stifled emotions bubbled to the surface. Loretta did not like Sally, because she'd overheard her saying nasty things about Mom when Sally thought there was no one else on the phone. Rose did not like Sally, because when Sally moved in, she took down Rose's mother's chandelier from the dining room, and it could not be found. Rose also accused Sally of taking her mother's religious statues that were stored in the attic, a place that Sally was told was off limits to her since our personal items were stored there. Since Sally had so much "stuff," she needed more room for storage and thus violated the attic space.

This upset Rose so much that she could not talk directly to Sally, even if they were standing next to each other. Rose would say, "Tell Sally that she took my mother's statues and that I want them back." (Some curse words have been omitted.) Vinny would have to relay the message.

Loretta and Rose were both upset that Sally's rent, at $800, was half the going rate. They thought that I had negotiated that rate, but, in fact, it was my mother and her friend Mary who sealed that arrangement. Neither I nor Sally were to blame.

Since we were the landlords and owned the house, Loretta and Rose demanded we give Sally orders to leave the property by October 15 and tell her that she would have to comply. This was theoretically true, but in the real world in New York, it does not work that way. If Sally decided not to move, we would have to evict her, which I did not want to do. It could take months or longer, especially since there was a child involved. I thought our best course of action, in a spirit of cooperation, was to help pay Sally's moving expenses. I thought this would entice her to move, since, one way or another, she would be moving. If we could get her to stick to the buyer's timetable, we could sell the house before the winter and avoid a possible roof collapse or worse.

Rose and Loretta vehemently opposed paying Sally's moving expenses; it was a difficult discussion, but they eventually agreed. Sally wanted to move to her mother's house, around the corner from Mom's house. She had life rights to an apartment and a yard at the house where she could plant flowers, but the probate of her mom's estate was not yet complete. She was embroiled in a legal dispute with her stepchildren, who wanted to sell the house and give Sally part of the proceeds in lieu of the life rights. Sally wanted the life rights. Vinny had a method for checking if the probate had been settled, which he checked every day. Sally did not want to move out of our house and move again when her mother's estate was settled, so settlement was important to us in order to make the October 15th closing date.

Me as We (Relationships and Married Life)

Vinny and Rose became friends with the buyers and asked if the closing date could be moved to October 30th, giving us an additional two weeks. The buyers agreed.

We asked Aunt Sarah, Mom's sister-in-law, if she would accompany us to Arizona to assist in Mom's relocation; we would pay her plane fare. Since she was always willing to help and her daughter lived in Arizona, she agreed. The one problem was that Aunt Sarah received weekly shots for a medical problem, and we were not sure if that could take place in Arizona. We made these arrangements. We made the plane reservations for October 22nd to coincide with Loretta returning home from vacation. Mom no longer had a valid driver's license, and her passport had expired, so we were not sure what proof of ID we needed. When we called the airport, they said we could use her expired driver's license. Was this true? We would find out with certainty at the airport.

We had a car pick up Aunt Sarah from her house and bring her to Mom's house in Brooklyn on October 21st, the day before our departure. Aunt Sarah packed for Mom. It was a difficult packing assignment, since Mom was not returning. What do you take, and how do you tell Mom she's going on vacation when she didn't really want to go?

On **October 22,** a car picked up Savia and me at our home in New Jersey and drove us to Mom's house in Brooklyn. Mom did not want to leave her house. We told her that Loretta was moving and that she wanted her there to help. The house needed to be worked on, and it would take a few months, so mom could spend the winter in Arizona with Loretta. She reluctantly came along. Fortunately, Mom's expired ID was acceptable.

Savia and I spent a week in Arizona with Loretta, Aunt Sarah, and Mom. We did some sightseeing and went to the butterfly museum. It was great to see Mom having fun. While we were in Arizona, Vinny called with the good news that Sally's mother's estate had been settled and that Sally could now move in. I called Sally and told her the news even before her attorney called her. Mom spent the rest of her days in Arizona, near Loretta.

On **October 24,** while Savia and I were in Arizona, Rose and Vinny were removing items they wanted from the Brooklyn house. Tara, Pasquale, and Daria also went to pack glassware and put clothes in plastic bags. House cleaning was a team effort. Vinny was able to negotiate another extension for the house closing, to November 13.

Between **October 29 and November 2,** when Savia and I were back in Brooklyn, we continued emptying the house. We had three piles — garbage, recycle, and keep. Since the garbage and recycle had to be placed at the curb the morning before pickup and because it was too much for Sally to move, we loaded it into my car and brought it back to New Jersey to dispose of. I never thought I would have to import garbage and recyclables, since I had plenty of my own!

Sally looked like she needed help to meet the closing deadline of November 13th. This was an important date to us, since we did not want to lose the buyer, start all over again with showing the house and negotiations, and miss selling the house before winter. And if Sally changed her mind, all was lost.

Sally, understandably, wanted her mom's house ready before she moved in. That meant moving unwanted furniture out and painting the rooms. We hired 1-800-JUNK for $1,600 to remove the unwanted furniture and junk from Sally's mom's house. Although it was not part of the moving expenses, we thought it was reasonable to pay this. The handyman she hired

Me as We (Relationships and Married Life)

appeared to not be able to finish in time for the furniture to be moved in prior to closing, so I met with him. I asked him what it would take to finish on time. He said, "If I can hire two more guys to help me, I am sure it will be finished on time, but I would have to pay them about $400." I agreed and paid him the additional funds. He actually did finish on time; however, he did not hire the extra people. I did not realize that Brooklyn was New York's Sicily and that honesty and integrity were things found only in an old dusty dictionary.

Sally called us at home at night and said she did not think she could be packed and ready to leave by the deadline of November 12th. Savia calmed her nerves and convinced her that it could happen and that we would help.

Sally and her granddaughter were in the process of packing, but the clutter was unimaginable. It appeared that anything Sally ever touched during her lifetime had been randomly stored throughout the house. In each room, there was a pile for moving, a pile for donating, and a pile for garbage. The worst area was the third floor, where my Aunt Jo used to live with the accompanying attic. Savia and I helped with this area. We wore gloves, hats, and masks for dust protection in the attic and slowly went through each item, determining if it was Aunt Rose's or Sally's and asking which pile it should go in. Savia and I took days off from work to get this accomplished.

The next step was to move Sally's furniture from Mom's house to Sally's mother's house around the block. After giving us an estimate of $1,400, the moving company came on **November 11** to move the furniture and boxed items. We agreed to also pay this bill for Sally. The moving people, however, said they would not take the massive amount of unboxed items. We called College Hunks, who would remove these items for $665. We did not have our checkbooks with us, and credit cards were not acceptable, so Sally paid this bill, although we said that we would reimburse her.

On **November 12,** College Hunks was to come to remove the final items from the house. Vinny asked if I could be there with him for this last day. I had just been appointed the Treasurer of my homeowner's association, and that date was the night of the first meeting, which I couldn't miss. So, I was not able to accompany Vinny. That was a mistake. After all we'd been through, I should have been there to seal the house closing with Vinny.

On that day, Vinny's son Richard was there to help. They removed more items from the house, and when they went to remove the improperly installed window air conditioner for Sally, it fell out the second-story window and smashed to the ground.

At the end of a long day, Richard had to leave, while Vinny remained in the house, which was still not empty. Clothing and trash were still everywhere, and the next morning was the walk-through with the buyers. Sally's granddaughter's friends came to the house and verbally — almost physically — threatened Vinny to leave the house open for them to remove the remaining items the next morning. This was not possible. Vinny did the only thing possible to secure the house for the early morning walk-through: he nailed a board across the inside of the front door to the house to prevent entry. With tears in his eyes, thinking of all our relatives who'd lived in the house and how shocked they would be to see him having to board up the front door, he left for his New Jersey home through the exit in Mom's house.

Me as We (Relationships and Married Life)

On **November 13, the day of the closing,** Vinny walked the buyers through the house, explaining what had transpired the night before. They were disappointed that there was still some trash in the house, but they said it would not interfere with the closing.

I promised to pay Sally the $665 she'd lent me to pay College Hunks to remove the unboxed items. Because she'd given Vinny such a hard time at the end, with her friends threatening him, I wondered if I should still pay her.

On **November 22,** a week after the closing, I wrote the check out for $665, put it in an envelope and addressed it to Sally's new address. If Loretta, Vinny, and Rose knew that I'd even considered sending Sally a check, they would have been horrified after the way Vinny had been treated. I did make a promise. I went to the post office to pick up my mail, but something told me not to mail the check.

I was spending the day at my daughter's house when I received a call from Vinny. The outside temperature was 28° when Vinny went to the house with the buyers; it was extremely cold inside the house. The first thing he did was to go upstairs to examine the only thermostat in the house and found it missing. That's when he called me. I said, "Look around and see if you can find it. Perhaps, as the furniture was being moved, it could have hit the thermostat and knocked it off the wall." I held the phone, waiting to hear. He couldn't find the thermostat anywhere and directed his attention to a hole in the wall; he determined that the wires had a clean cut, meaning intentionally cut. If it had been a colder day, the water pipes in the house could have frozen. That's when I knew that I'd made the right decision not to return the $665 to Sally.

A Blessed and Guided Life

Timeline for move and house closing

Oct 15	Wednesday	Loretta leaves for vacation
Oct 19	Sunday	Visit Mom and remove or list items to keep - Savia, Bob, Daria, Tara
		Pack large suitcase for Mom and bring home
Oct 21	Tuesday	Loretta returns from vacation
		Check on computer for boarding passes
		Aunt Sarah goes to Mom's house; pickup 12 noon by Serenity Limousine
Oct 22	Wednesday	Plane Flight Newark to Arizona – Mom, Bob, Savia, Aunt Sarah
		US Airways Flight 660 leaves 1:55 PM; arrives 4:01 PM
		Car Rental for Arizona – done
		Car picks up Savia and Bob 7:45 AM in Randolph, NJ; bring to Brooklyn
		Car takes all of us to Newark airport; need wheelchair and Mom's ID
Oct 24	Friday	Aunt Sarah – shot at doctors 9:30 AM Aunt Sarah at Loretta's
		7373N. Scottsdale Rd. Bldg. E Scottsdale
		Vinny and Rose remove items from Brooklyn house they want to keep
Oct 26	Sunday	Tara and Pasquale to pack glasses and put clothes in plastic bags
Oct 27	Monday	Plane Flight from Arizona to Newark - Bob and Savia
		US Airways Flight 683 leaves 3:25 PM; arrives 11:01 PM
Oct 29	Wednesday	Bob and Savia visit Brooklyn house and remove what they want
Oct 30	Thursday	
Oct 31	Friday	Aunt Sarah – shot at doctors 9:30 AM
Nov 2	Sunday	Bob and Savia visit Brooklyn house and remove what they want
Nov 4	Tuesday	Voting Day Aunt Sarah at Liz's
		Furniture pickup
Nov 7	Friday	Aunt Sarah – shot at doctors 9:30 AM
		Furniture pickup 2
Nov 13	Thursday	**Brooklyn House Closing – The Big Day!**
Nov 14	Friday	Aunt Sarah – shot at doctors 9:30 AM
Nov 16	Sunday	Plane Flight Newark to Arizona – Aunt Sarah
		US Airways Flight 687 leaves 9:45 AM; arrives 4:23 PM
		Bob and Savia to bring Aunt Sarah to her home in Long Island

Aide stays with Mom from October 27th onward

Bob and Savia staying here:
Best Western
7515 E. Butherus Drive
Scottsdale, AZ 85260

Me as We (Relationships and Married Life)

After sending in my deposit for the roof in October 2013 and finishing the roof in June of 2014, I received a call from the owner of Branch Restoration in August 2015 asking to be paid. I told him that I had made a total of five calls and emails asking for the bill and warranty, so that I could pay the bill. He said, "If I send you the warranty, you may not pay the bill." I said, "If I pay the bill, you may not send me the warranty." I think we both had reasonable skepticism. We decided he would send me an email copy of the warranty, I would pay the bill, and then he would send me the original. That's what happened.

I would not think that a stray shingle lying in Mom's front yard would have resulted in this cascade of events. Mom was being well taken care of, the house was sold before the winter, and life seemed to be back to normal again.

Mohonk Adventure
A Close Call

"Can I have two keys to our room, one that works and another that doesn't?" I asked the receptionist. She didn't ask why, and I didn't tell. It was June of 2015, and the trees were in full splendor, especially at this elevation. This landmark resort had been founded in 1869 and had everything—great food, swimming pool, spa, a beach, rowing, pitch and putt course, and horseback riding. And don't forget afternoon teatime. But best of all was the scenery. It was built on a quarry that was later filled with water. There were ground-level and elevated trails that rambled through the rocks and forest.

After I gave Gabriella and Sophia their room keys, they ran yelling and screaming through the halls to see if they could find the room first and who had the working key. This was our routine each time we visited the Mohonk Mountain House.

When hiking day came, we decided to take the elevated trail that overlooks the lake and hotel. It was even more beautiful from that vantage point. In several areas surrounding the lake, there were little wooden gazebos built on rock that jutted out into the lake to enhance your view. The perimeter of the viewing area had tree-branch fences.

As we left our elevated trail, there was a narrow wooden bridge that connected the trail to the gazebo. Gabriella crossed the bridge and was standing on the rock waiting for Sophia. Sophia was a little anxious about crossing the narrow bridge. I was in front of her, so I gave her my hand to guide her as I crossed the bridge backward. We both crossed the bridge, but, since I was facing Sophia, I could not tell that the adjoining rock surface sloped down toward the lake. If I'd been facing forward, it wouldn't have been a problem. But who crosses the bridge going backward?

Me as We (Relationships and Married Life)

I lost my balance and started tumbling toward the branch-made fence. I was picking up some speed and hit the fence with considerable force. Fortunately, I am not a big person, and the fence was able to stop me from falling over the cliff onto the rocks below.

I could see why they say, "Thin people live longer." However, people who walk forward live the longest.

From Bikes to Buses
Bermuda Trip 2018

Bermuda is our favorite place on the planet. In January of 2017, I said to Savia, "How about we go to Bermuda?" Her instant reply was a loud and smiling "Yes!" Although we had been there six times before, our last trip had been 15 years ago. We love the feeling of serenity on the island, the beaches, the aquamarine clear water, and the flowers, but most of all, we loved the motorbikes. Savia and I had spent our honeymoon in Bermuda. I drove while she sat behind me, reading the street map. We felt safe visiting every street on the island as the wind blew through our hair.

Let me explain our passion for motorbikes. When Daria and Tara were in their late teens, we took them to Bermuda, so that they could experience the island and the motorbikes as we had. Before you are allowed to rent a bike in Bermuda, you have to pass a basic stability test. The Bermudians hate to see splattered tourists on their streets. Each of us took the test. Savia was stable for a while but then ran into the hedges; Daria stopped the bike in the middle of the test; Tara drove OK but was deemed not stable enough. I was the only one who passed the test. So, everywhere we went, I had to make three trips each way. I loved it, but the girls were disappointed.

When we arrived home, we bought a motorbike and practiced until we were all excellent riders. We had to be stable and confident enough to ride on the opposite side of the street, and we were. When we went back to Bermuda two years later, Daria and Tara had their own bikes, while Savia was my passenger, as usual. We had a great time riding around the island and even passed a five-foot-high wall of blooming, vibrant red hibiscus, whose color tickled your eyes as you passed.

So now we decided to visit Bermuda again. Because hotels there are expensive, Daria and Tara suggested that we consider an Airbnb for our next trip. After a few days of surfing the internet, we found one we thought was suitable. It had a pool; the owners lived next door; there were two chairs overlooking the ocean; it was a mile from Whole Foods and half a mile from an organic farm and grocery store; it was one third the price of the hotel. We emailed that we would like to book the place. The reply indicated that there would be a response within 48 hours. About 30 seconds later, we received a response from the owners, Richard and Karen, welcoming us to their place in Bermuda.

About a month before the trip, Daria and Tara said that there was a new mode of transportation on the island called a "Twizzy." It was a cross between a motorbike and a small car. Only Bermuda residents could drive a car in Bermuda, but this vehicle was an exception. They thought this might be a safer choice for us compared to a motorbike, because Bermuda was a British territory, and you had to drive on the opposite side of the street. We told them it sounded great and that we would rent the Twizzy. However, when we called to reserve it, we discovered that, since this was new to the island and there were not many available, there was a nine-month waiting list. A motorbike had been our first choice anyway, so we felt the decision had already been made for us.

We called Richard two weeks before our trip to iron out some details. He said that, since his place was a little out of the way, not all taxi drivers could find it. He said that his regular driver, Vincent, would pick us up at the airport, take us to his place, and would be available whenever we needed him. That sounded great. What service!

Finally, the day came, and we arrived at the Bermuda airport. There was an unusually long wait to go through customs. Vincent met us after we passed through customs but said that, because we had been delayed, he couldn't take us to our place. But he said not to worry — he would hand us off to someone reliable after explaining the directions to them. Off we went. It was a 45-minute ride from the airport, and our new driver had some difficulty finding the place, even with Vincent's directions. It was about $80 cash. Credit cards

A Blessed and Guided Life

were not accepted. Our vacation apartment was connected to the owner's home. It had a living room/dining room, kitchen, and bedroom. They seemed to have thought of everything. They had a cell phone for us with their phone numbers in it, phone numbers for restaurants and Vincent, the driver's, phone number. In the kitchen was a book with a list of points of interest, phone numbers, and taxi services. But best of all were the two chairs on the cliff high above the aquamarine ocean water. It was so relaxing and peaceful that you could just sit there for hours. Eventually, we realized we had to eat. Just then, Richard came by from next door and asked if we had done any food shopping. When we told him we had not, he offered to drive us to the market. We accepted. He spoke to the shoppers as we gathered our groceries and then drove us back to the apartment. From the main road, it was

Me as We (Relationships and Married Life)

a mile uphill over a winding gravel road before you reached the apartment. We had dinner that evening and breakfast the next morning, oftentimes sitting in the chairs overlooking the ocean. The next day happened to be "Bermuda Day." It seems that, in Bermuda, there is always some special day going on — a parade or some other reason to celebrate. We made reservations for 1:30 p.m. at the restaurant in town so we could view the parade, which started at 2 p.m. We called a taxi that would pick us up at 12:30, so we would have plenty of time to get to town. 12:30 p.m. came and went. 12:45 p.m. also came and went. We called the number of the taxi service, and of course, there was no answer. We called Vincent, the reliable driver recommended by Richard and Karen. He answered the phone but said he was busy for the entire week. We had been counting on him to get us to not only the parade but also to lunch and take-home dinner. Now what?

We went next door and told Richard that we had reservations at the restaurant at 1:30 and asked if he knew any other reliable taxi services. He said it was not 1:30, as we thought, but 2:30. We'd used the cell phone he gave us to determine the time. Somehow the cell phone was wrong. We were already an hour late for our restaurant. The restaurant owner knew Richard and said not to worry — he would have a table for us. Richard drove us near the restaurant, and we walked the rest of the way, since the roads were blocked from traffic during the all-day parade. It was a hot day, and everyone was under huge tents on the sidewalk along the parade route. Our table in the restaurant was in front of a large window, where we had a great view of the parade while taking advantage of the air conditioning. We actually had the best seat in the house or outside. We spent several hours watching the parade and eating an excellent lunch in the air-conditioned restaurant. Toward the end of the day, we had to locate a taxi to take us back.

The area was still blocked from traffic. We were told that there were two places we could get a taxi back to our apartment. One was only a few blocks away, and the second was farther down the next street — a considerable walk. Weaving and bobbing, we meandered through the crowds until we arrived at a more isolated location, where there was a taxi stand. We waited for about 15 minutes, with no sign of a taxi. We decided to try the second location. Again, after a long walk, no luck. In the distance, we could see the Hamilton Princess Hotel, our last chance and best hope for a ride back. We were walking in the middle of the street, and after only one block, we literally walked into a taxi that was just standing there. The woman driver said she had been waiting by the hotel for a long time, had given up, and decided to drive around. Fortunately, we could explain to her how to find our apartment.

We had breakfast the next day at the apartment. We did not expect to be taking taxis that accepted only cash, so our funds were getting low. We asked Richard for another favor. Could he drive us to the motorbike-rental place only about two miles away? He gladly agreed. We also told him that Vincent told us he was occupied; the lack of transportation forced us to use taxis, and we were running out of money. He generously offered to lend us $300. These people did everything they possibly could to make our stay with them more pleasant. He also said that we could take the bus to The Reefs Hotel, a short distance from the apartment, and could take a taxi from there. Why hadn't we thought of that? *Thump!* That is the sound of the palm of my hand smacking my forehead.

Me as We (Relationships and Married Life)

He drove us to the motorbike-rental place, which was across the street from The Reefs Hotel. I thought that, if we rented the bike, I could drive Savia up the hill to the apartment. The bike attendant gave me a helmet and instructions for operating the bike. The road that was used for the test drive was a narrow two-lane-wide side road with almost no traffic. I started the bike and cautiously and timidly drove down the road. The U-turn to come back proved a challenge. There was a cinder-block wall at the end that I narrowly missed because I was applying the gas and brake at the wrong times. The attendant drove his bike down to determine my status. He said, "Would you like some more practice and then try it again?" I said, "No" and failed myself. I thought riding the motorbike was a given. I hadn't realized that, after 15 years, I may have changed, and the traffic was far worse. I also was aware that I had to drive on the opposite side and that I would have Savia on the back seat. I could picture a disaster.

We walked across the street to the bus stop and went to the Southampton Princess Hotel to do some souvenir shopping and eat. Our stay at the apartment was too stressful, so we decided to relocate to a hotel. The Southampton Princess had no vacancies, but they did call many other hotels for us. All of them were booked full, as well. A taxi took us back to our apartment. The one hotel the Southampton did not call was The Reefs, because they did not have the number. We called when we got back, and fortunately there was a three-night opening in two days. We jumped at the chance.

The next morning, we told Richard and Karen that we were grateful that they had done all they could possibly do to make our trip enjoyable; but we made it clear that the transportation was not working out and that we were moving to a hotel. We also conceded that it was not their fault that Savia could not walk to the bus, the taxis could not find their house, and I could not drive the motorbike or rent a Twizzy. We paid them as if we had stayed there the entire time.

We returned the money they had lent us, since the hotel was now our new source of funds. Richard graciously drove us to the hotel. As I said, they had done everything they could for us.

We checked in at The Reefs, ate there, took the bus many places, and enjoyed ourselves. As we were walking on the street outside the hotel, a young couple passed on a motorbike. Savia yelled out to them, "Enjoy it while you can!"

It was still a great trip, but experiencing Bermuda without a motorbike is like vacationing in one of the most beautiful places in the world blindfolded.

A Holiday to Remember
It was Up to Us 2020

"Grab the flag hanging outside the garage door—all the smaller flags, too—and put them in the car," Savia called out to me. I loaded the car, and we drove to Daria's house dressed in the most patriotic clothes we could find. Savia and I both had red, white, and blue shirts with blue pants. This was a celebration for which we wanted to dress appropriately. The sky was a clear blue and 80 degrees.

We arrived at Daria's house and found Daria, Erik, Tara, and the kids all dressed for the occasion, too. Pasquale was home with Siena. Some of us were a little nervous, others were excited, and some were embarrassed to take part in our event. When I first mentioned my idea to Savia, she said, "Are you

Me as We (Relationships and Married Life)

kidding? We can't do that." Then, when she saw how excited Daria was about the idea, she said she would join in.

Outside Daria's house, we decided who should be holding which flag, the order of the marchers, who would be in charge of the music, who would be doing the reading, and the route we would take through the streets of Madison, New Jersey. A few rounds of practice was all we needed.

We wondered how this would be received. Would we be booed, humiliated, arrested? We didn't care—we just wanted to celebrate the tradition.

We drove to our first block. The paraders, Daria, Tara, Erik, Gabriella, Sophia, Domenick, and Chez took their assigned places in line carrying their flags. Savia, being in charge of the music, stayed in the car with the sunroof opened and all windows down blasting the "Battle Hymn of the Republic" through the car speakers.

As we approached the first "target" house, one of Daria's friends, we noticed the family outside waiting for us. They were thrilled to see our group march up the street to their house with the accompanying music. When we reached their property, Domenick held the Declaration of Independence scroll as I read the first few lines through Daria's megaphone. Daria's friend, Marissa, said her father would be back in about 30 minutes and would have loved to see our performance, so we returned for an encore.

We drove to the next house, the Joneses'. Again, they were outside waiting for us. They appreciated our performance so much, they asked if they could join. We welcomed the company, as our group grew by five members. They brought their flags, and we marched through the streets around their block. The remainder of the "target-houses" involved car rides. Our new, larger group drove to the next house while singing an inspiring patriotic song at maximum volume down Main Street with the megaphone through the opened sunroof. We passed people smiling, giving us thumbs-up and cheering that we had brought the July 4th parade, although on a smaller scale, back to Madison, dispelling any doubts that the decision to put it on ourselves was a mistake. In July 2020, the Covid-19 virus scare had canceled the celebration, which we felt was unjustified, so we thought the tradition should continue. Let it go down in history that we participated in the parade—our own.

An Extraordinary Trip to the Post Office
Angels at Work

When Savia and I built our house in 1990, we'd already had a home business for eight years. Since back then, Savia was

Me as We (Relationships and Married Life)

at the post office almost every day to send packages and mail to clients. We felt we did not want a mailbox along with the obligatory shoveling and occasional reinstalling after it was knocked down by mischievous teenagers. A post office box was our solution.

During our recent family vacation to Tennessee, we shared a cold that ran through the family. After two weeks, Erik, my son-in-law, and I were the only ones who still had a persistent cough. My doctor, Dr. Weiss, said it was not bronchitis, not pneumonia and not Covid but probably a bacteria that had settled in my lungs. Knowing I take medicine as a last resort (my family and I are vehemently against drugs), he suggested some other options. However, if my gradual improvement did not stop, he gave me a prescription for antibiotics.

On July 28, 2021, I was home from work, even though I was not contagious. Continual coughing did not seem appropriate around other people.

After dropping off cardboard boxes at the recycling center and obtaining my prescription at the pharmacy, I thought I would go to the post office for the mail. I took the scenic, shorter route up Combs Avenue, a quiet little country road that passes the idyllic Miller's Hill Farm. I followed two dump trucks in my Honda Accord up the inclined road where we all stopped at the stop sign.

After a few moments, the dump truck in front of me put its backup lights on. I thought he was making room for the dump truck in front of him to slide back a little before starting up the hill. My assumption changed when the dump truck in front of me continued toward me. I tried putting my car in reverse but was too late. The truck smashed into the front of my car turning it sideways on the road and then rolled over on its side to the right of my car. The first dump truck, whose brakes had failed, now had clear access for a direct hit on my car. He was also picking up speed and was barreling toward the side of my car. I braced for the impact. It was like bumper cars with a 40-ton truck! Little did I know it was filled with sand! Would I wake up in this life or the next?

Opening my eyes after the impact, I saw glass everywhere. My right hand was bleeding in most places although coagulation had already begun. From the driver's seat, I could see that half the front windshield was mangled and that the other half was gone. The side airbag was visible, but I could see only truck metal out of the driver's window; the top of the car was smashed, leaving little room for me. There was some netting around the entire passenger side of the car. And where did all this sand come from?!

I heard voices outside and told the people I was alive and conscious. I heard them say that the situation was unstable. I didn't know if that meant my car might continue to be crushed or a fire might start. John McAndrew, the owner and farmer at Miller's Farm, brought his backhoe to position between my car and the falling truck to prevent any further crushing, but the police officer asked him not to engage since he thought any change in the delicate balance of forces might be "detrimental." I'm not sure why the truck did not descend further. Was it the sand, the position of the other truck, the Hand of God? Whatever it was, I am thoroughly grateful. Of course, I was anxious to escape the car.

The steering wheel and my seat left me almost no breathing room. I don't think the police knew how to get me out of the car. Doors could not open since they were surrounded by sand up to the windows. All windows were blocked or crushed.

Me as We (Relationships and Married Life)

The only possibility was the rear passenger window. I asked the police officer, Officer Hertzberg, the first responder at the scene, to break the back passenger window, and I would see if I could get there by climbing out. The netting that was previously covering the sand in the truck was now surrounding my car. The Fire Chief used the officer's knife to cut through the netting. The officer broke the window as I looked away and then placed a blanket on the bottom of the window to shield me from the remaining broken glass. Although the steering wheel was a few inches from my chest, I managed to release my seat belt and get up in my seat in a contorted position. I looked for the antibiotics I had just picked up from the pharmacy but could not find them. I made my way between the two front seats through the fragments of broken glass to the rear window. The officer asked me to put out my hands so he could pull me out of the window. When I was halfway out, I remember thinking, *Wouldn't it be a shame, after all this, if the truck came down now and took off my legs?* Fortunately, that didn't happen, and I was pulled to safety.

I was sitting on the side of the road when the police pointed the EMT people in my direction. They said, "He was the one in the car." Their response was, "What car?" With two dump trucks engulfing my car, which was covered in sand, it was difficult to tell that there even *was* a car.

I went to the ambulance for further evaluation. My blood pressure was extremely high—I was told that it is expected in trauma like this, but I was also in danger of a stroke. The blood pressure eventually decreased but still was a cause for concern. The EMT, Holly Flanagan, was with me the whole time. I called Savia using her phone and told her I was in a car accident but was OK and was being brought to the ER at Morristown just to make sure. Off to the Emergency Room at Morristown Memorial Hospital I went. Holly summarized the situation to the ER while en route as follows: "I have a male, age 74, who was in a car accident where two dump trucks

Me as We (Relationships and Married Life)

tried to crush him and almost succeeded. He has lacerations to his right hand. EKG looks good, blood pressure was 217 over 100, but has now decreased to 183 over 95. We are 15 minutes out." After the doctor examined my hand for glass fragments, and after chest, hip, back, and hand X-rays, I was released.

Voluntarily, Officer Hertzberg went to the impound lot and brought back my cell phone and any personal items he could find. The police, fire, and rescue squad are absolutely underappreciated. They risk their lives every day to help others. What an amazing calling!

There were still some items in the crushed car that I was hoping to recover. The next day, Savia and I went to the police impound lot. I walked in and said that my car had been brought there yesterday. The owner responded, "Are you the one who ordered the sand?" They said he'd been waiting all day for me just so he could deliver that line!

I think this was a dramatic sign that it was not time to take antibiotics. Is that the moral?

God is not finished with me here. He went through an awful lot to save me. I have to determine what my remaining purpose is and make it worth His while.

Around the Town
Community Service

While at the Randolph Town Fair, I met the Town Mayor. She asked if I would consider serving on one of the town committees. I agreed to look at the choices and see where I might be able to contribute. The Open Space Committee piqued my interest. After all, I'd scored high with Forest Ranger in my aptitude test, and I did like the outdoors. Our job was to identify open space in my town of Randolph and determine if it was a candidate for purchase and preserving it as open space. It had to be a large-enough area for a park or sports fields and needed to be contiguous (That's a new word for me. It means "connected.") to existing open space. During my eight years on the committee, one-third of all land in Randolph was forever preserved from development. The building contractors were not fans of our work.

In 2014, the President of the Homeowners Association called and asked me if I was interested in serving on the Board of Directors as Treasurer. My responsibilities would be to receive and pay all the bills of the association, send out invoices for dues, keep track of delinquent payments, and prepare financial reports to the Board and homeowners. I had lived in Mendham Lake Estates for 24 years and had not participated in the management of the association, so I volunteered to do my part. The responsibilities were not difficult but did take more time than I anticipated. This was a two-year appointment, however, I was willing to hold this position indefinitely. There was one board member who wanted to be President. And at every meeting, he would try to intimidate and outright declare the current President incompetent. The stress and tension were more than I was willing to accept. When my two-year term was over, I did not ask for reappointment. This was a small sample of how personalities, egos, and politics work, and I wanted no part of it.

Unintended Consequences

One day, Daria and I were in Shoprite approaching the checkout area. I was sort of aimlessly walking around. We passed a sign that indicated "10 items or less," which was above a checkout station intended to serve shoppers who had only a

Me as We (Relationships and Married Life)

few grocery items. As we passed this sign, for some unknown reason, I read the sign out loud. "10 items or less." The woman ahead of us gathered up all her groceries, said, "Sorry," and walked away sheepishly. I was unaware of what I had caused until Daria explained it to me.

Another time, Savia and I were sitting in a restaurant when our chocolate mousse dessert arrived. I was excited to dig into my dessert and exclaimed loudly "mooooousse". Unbeknownst to me, a very large woman was passing by our table and Savia thought I was "moo-ing" at her! I hope she didn't hear me!

Who Am I?
Names

I always thought our family name, Giarraffa, referred to a giraffe. This seemed unusual, since, at that point, I was the tallest Giarraffa at 5 feet 7½ inches. When the internet became popular, it gave the curious additional reference tools. When I looked up the name "Giarraffa," it referenced a specialty olive grown in Sicily. This seemed a more likely heritage.

"Ralph" is not actually my middle name. I only *thought* it was. During the time I was studying for confirmation in the church, I took the name "Ralph" after my sponsor — my Uncle Ralph. I used this as my middle name for many years. It is even on my Social Security Card. I did not realize until I was 50 years old that I did not have a middle name. There was no middle name on my birth certificate. *Who knew!*

At 2:30 a.m., December 15, at age 71, I woke up and somehow was thinking about my first name. Some people call me "Robert," and others call me "Bob." How did that happen? Was it the cousins on Long Island who called me "Bob"? No, that wasn't it. In my head, I went through the voices of each relative, hearing them call my name — some "Robert," some "Bob." Then, I broke the code. I could hear my father's voice: "I named you 'Robert.' That's your name." All the relatives on my father's side of the family call me "Robert," while all the relatives on my mother's side of the family call me "Bob." How is it that I did not uncover this mystery or even knew that it existed until I was 71? Isn't it odd that the mother and father have different names for the child? What other puzzles lurk behind the scenes?

Even though I arrived early, the line to register for the Brian Tracy Goals Seminar was still significant. When the girl in front of me took her turn to register, she said her name was "Lisa Giarraffa." The person registering her asked her to spell her last name. It was exactly the same as mine. I was surprised but did not want to interrupt her registration process. However, I did want to speak to her to see if we were related. It is rare that I meet a "Giarraffa" that I don't know. Correction: not "rare" — *never.*

I waited until my registration was over and then started to look for her. The seminar location was arranged with about 25 exhibit booths before the main entrance; there were rows of folding chairs, totaling about 500. I searched each exhibit booth to see if I could find her. No luck. Where could she have gone? I scanned the seating area to see if I could locate her, to no avail. I must have missed her at the exhibit booth. It was close to the start of the meeting, and I wanted a seat near the front, so I put my book and jacket on a folding chair in the third row and went back to the exhibit area to search some more. How could she have disappeared? I knew it wasn't my imagination. The seminar was starting, so I went back to

Me as We (Relationships and Married Life)

my seat and was surprised to see Lisa Giarraffa sitting right next to me. During break, I explained that I'd overheard her name at registration, and we tried to connect our family trees — again, to no avail. Perhaps if we go back deep enough in the roots, a connection could be found. What are the chances of me being next to her during registration and then her randomly sitting next to me? One in 500 times one in 500, which is one out of 250,000. Definitely possible but very unusual. Not sure what the moral of this story is, but I thought it an interesting attempt at a search for ancestors.

Joe Okaly, my unofficial adopted son by mutual agreement, called me and said that he had been to the Turtle Back Zoo, which he often visits with his wife, Lauren, and their 1,000-day-old daughter, Avery. Yes, I keep track of the days and send out milestone announcements. They were feeding a giraffe at the zoo, and they started talking to the zookeeper. It seems that, of the entire family of giraffes there, they were feeding the tallest giraffe. The zookeeper said the giraffe's name was "Robert," but all the zoo workers called him "Bob" — a true story.

A Blessed and Guided Life

Joseph, Noah, Lauren and Avery Okaly

Mini-Me (My Children and Grandchildren)

Children

After six years of marriage, it was time for our first child. We'd had such a wonderful six years that we were a little anxious about how a new child would change our lives. We liked the name "Daria" — coincidentally, Savia's father's name was "Dario" although that is not why we chose the name. We did not want to insult my father, Domenick, so we thought that, if Daria's middle name was "Monique," a derivative of "Domenick," it would somehow lessen our anxiety. We thought that, if you said "Daria Monique" quickly, it would sound like "Domenick." That is how she got her name. When Savia started labor, she was almost ready to go to the hospital. But first, she had to make a sandwich for me to bring. She was at the kitchen counter making the sandwich when she started having contractions. Three times, I would roll a chair under her so she could sit down until the pains passed, and then she would resume making the sandwich. On July 23, 1977, one day early, Daria was born. She was already considerate, arriving on a Saturday. Our anxiety about how a baby would change our lives was unnecessary. Life was even better.

On June 16, 1979, Tara was born, one day later than expected. That made one day early and one day late — overall, exactly on time. There were two names that we liked, "Tara" and "Diana." At the last moment at the hospital, "Tara" won out. "Jean" just sounded like it went together with "Tara," and there you go. She was also very considerate being born on Saturday so I would not have to miss much work.

Savia nursed both children but started supplementing in the third month with Enfamil or Soy Lac. I mention that because my Aunt Jo called Savia and asked if she was using a soy-based baby formula that was in the news. It appeared that the manufacturer had neglected to add sodium to the formula, the absence of which caused brain damage to many infants. If Tara had been exclusively bottle fed, who knows where she would be today? When there is a choice, go natural.

The girls grew up in our split-level home in a friendly, warm community on Sanford Drive in Randolph. We had a corner lot that felt like it was an acre of land. There was a garden in the back where Daria and Tara picked vegetables. They enjoyed playing with their friends in their very own Garden of Eden.

When the girls were growing up, we had three quirks unique to us that I would like to tell you about. The first was "calibrated hands." When you think your child is sick with fever, you take their temperature. But before you take their temperature, you feel their forehead and make a judgement as to whether it is normal or high. I wanted to refine the

Mini-Me (My Children and Grandchildren)

"normal or high" guess, so I designed a system to do that. I felt my child's forehead, guessed the temperature, and then took the temperature to see how close I was. After many, many trials using that system, I was able to estimate the actual temperature +/– 0.2 degrees. It is amazing what you can do with practice.

The second was The Heisenberg Uncertainty Principle, which I learned in school. It states that it is impossible to know simultaneously the exact position and momentum of a particle. *This is because when you measure one, you interfere with the other.*

I taught this principle to my children but in an extrapolated way for which it was probably not intended. The Giarraffa Corollary to the Heisenberg Uncertainty Principle is "If you know you are being observed, you will take that into consideration and act differently."

For example, when we wanted my father to pose for a photo, we might call out "Heisenberg," because his posed smile was different than his candid smile. If the chiropractor asks you to walk down the hall to observe your gait, it may not be your normal walk. We used this principle often to explain abnormal behavior due to observation.

The third quirk was our unit of measure. It began when we were crossing the Verrazano Bridge and the girls asked the question, "How many Bernie's deep is the water?" I took a wild guess and told them 30. My cousin Bernie Tuosto was the tallest one in the family at six feet, two inches. From then on, any great distance was measured in "Bernies." Now, with the help of the internet, it is easy to look up the depth of the water under the bridge. It is actually 28 Bernies deep. Good guess.

When Daria was 13 years old, we were standing on the front lawn at Canterbury Court. She looked across the street and said, "Why does the grass across the street look so beautiful and full, when ours looks spotty?" "Good question," I said. I took her hand, and we walked across the street and stood on our neighbor's lawn. From there, the opposite looked true. I told her to remember this. This is true not only of lawns but of many other areas of life. I was familiar with the expression but never actually tried it in real life until that day.

When Daria graduated from high school, she asked if a graduation gift could be a trip to Italy. She had been there once before, when she was seven.

Daria and Tara both studied Italian in college and were fairly fluent. They both spent five months in Italy in a study-abroad program. Daria went first. She went to purchase clothes, since the airline had lost her luggage, but the people in Florence were not her shape or size. Things were not going too well for her, so she would call every day asking to come home. She studied the bus route and then went exploring, thinking that this would be her only chance to see Italy before coming home. Savia finally talked her into staying. Daria was the only one there from her school, so she knew no one. During the three months she was there, she made many friends, including Erik, a classmate, who was also the only one there from his school. At the time, Daria was dating someone from her college, but when that ended, Erik, who lived only 15 minutes away back home, stepped in. They had to travel 4,000 miles to Florence, Italy, to meet. Three years later, they were married. A coincidence?

Tara arrived in Siena three weeks after Daria, so their time in Italy overlapped. They were a one-hour bus ride from

Mini-Me (My Children and Grandchildren)

each other and visited often. Tara made friends with a family in Siena, and we went to visit them several times.

When Tara started dating, she told her prospective boyfriends that she was not moving out of New Jersey. It began with a guy from Alabama she'd met. His family relocated to Belgium for work, resulting in a week-long visit for us. Then while studying abroad, Tara met a guy from Siena, Italy. He came here on a trial basis, but it didn't work out. However, his parents were so grateful that we'd helped their son that we made two trips to Siena with them as our tour guides of the city. We are still friends. Next for Tara was a guy from Michigan. He sold his house and moved to New Jersey for a while. It didn't work out, either. Then she dated a friend she'd met in school who lived in Indiana. That didn't work out, either, but she seemed to be getting closer to New Jersey. As Savia and I would lie in bed each night, we would laugh and say, "I wonder if this is the last of the "far-away people"?

Then it happened. When Tara had attended religious-education class as a child, the teacher would give the kids sugary treats during class. We did not want Tara eating sugar, so Savia told the teacher that she was allergic to sugar — everyone is, to some degree. The teacher changed her rewards, and Savia and she became lifelong friends. About 30 years later, the teacher's son introduced Tara to Pasquale, her "husband to be." Pasquale later asked me for Tara's hand in marriage. I said, "I have been waiting for you for 10 years. Where have you been?"

I can't possibly express how proud and privileged I am to be the father of two intelligent, considerate, and loving daughters.

A Blessed and Guided Life

Daria's Family

Tara's Family

Mini-Me (My Children and Grandchildren)

Grandchildren

This is how we announced our first Grandchild

Savia, 58; Mom, 83; Daria, 27, married; Tara, 26, single

The log flume ride in Disney World is a not-so-bad roller coaster ride up this steep incline, with a 50-foot drop through the water below. As you are on your way down, your picture is taken to capture your expression of exhilaration through the descent. When we went to view the photos at the gift shop, my entire family was wide-eyed and excited in the photo except for me. I seemed to be sitting there calmly, as if listening to a speech. After some thought, I came to the conclusion that everyone was participating in the experience, while I was "observing" the experience.

Not sure what to make of that. It did, however, remind me of the difference between being a parent and being a grandparent. You participate in being a parent, but you observe as a grandparent. Keeping this in mind, I tried to be more participatory. My goal is to teach each of my grandchildren how to ride a two-wheeler bike. I taught Gabriella and Sophia. Domenick, Chez, and Siena are left. Hopefully, they will all remember how they learned to ride.

Driving Gabriella and Sophia to School

During March of 2012, Daria and Erik were having some work done in their home in Madison. The contractor did a very poor job at leveling the basement floor and sanding the wood floors throughout the house. The newly poured cement in the basement cracked when you walked on it, and the sanding of the floors left uneven gouges in the wood. The staining was also not uniform. This resulted in hiring a different contractor to fix the first contractor's mess. Overall, this took about two months. While this work was taking place at Daria and Erik's house, Daria and the girls stayed at Nana and PopPop's house in Randolph. Gabriella, age six, and Sophia, age three, still

Mini-Me (My Children and Grandchildren)

had to attend school a half-hour away in Madison. When I drove them to school, I had a bag of almonds in the car and thought they might like some. I asked the girls if they were allergic to nuts. Gabriella thought for a moment and said, "Yes, I am allergic to peanuts and donuts."

Gabriella wanted to be first in line at school. There were always one or two children who would consistently beat her to the spot. Our goal was to have Gabriella first in line. Every morning, Gabriella would get dressed, eat her breakfast, get her backpack ready, and be waiting to leave for school. We always left early, just in case the traffic was heavy. Every five minutes, she would ask, "What are the kids doing now? Are they out of bed yet? Are they dressed? Are they eating breakfast? Are they walking to school?" Except for one day when there was extra-heavy traffic, she was first. As each child arrived, you could see by her glimmering face how proud she was of her position in line.

Since I drove them to school each day, I thought this might be a good opportunity to add to their knowledge. I wanted to make them aware of things that they had seen every day but did not notice. We started with red Japanese maple trees by counting the number of trees between my house and their school and then seeing whose guess was closest. During the trip, we discussed that some trees lose their leaves in the winter, and some don't, the shape of the leaves, trees with symmetrical branches and trees with asymmetrical branches, the texture of the tree bark, the age of the trees, and what the wood is used for. They found it interesting and were asking questions. The next day, we discussed fire hydrants, their purpose, where the water came from, firehouses, and firemen. Again, how many were there between my house and their school? The next day, it was the American flag — who started it, why those colors, what the stars meant, what the stripes meant, and how many different flags there had been throughout American history. Other days, the topics were telephone poles, white picket fences, bricks, and electricity. When I ran out of topics, I asked them the day before what they wanted to learn about. We covered many other topics, including planets, stars, clouds, and lightning. It was not home schooling but car schooling. When summer came, and everyone was back home, Daria asked the girls what classes they would like to take and what they would like to learn. Gabriella said, "PopPop taught us everything already. We don't need any more classes."

Prologue to "The Visit"
One weekend each month, Daria would be away at Homeopathic School in Manhattan. On most of those weekends, we would take the children for a day or overnight to give Erik some free time. We tried to be creative to entertain them and have them learn at the same time. One morning, after breakfast, I asked them which fairy tales they knew. Did they know "Goldilocks and the Three Bears," "Little Red Riding Hood," or others? We made a list of the fairy tales we knew and what stood out in each tale. Then I asked them to make up a story using portions from as many fairy tales as they could. After initial contributions by Domenick and Sophia, Gabriella wrote "The Visit" in about 20 minutes.

"The Visit"
Once upon a time, in a galaxy far, far away, there lived a giant with very long golden hair who wore glass slippers. He had

Mini-Me (My Children and Grandchildren)

seven brothers. He rode in a pumpkin carriage to visit his grandmother for the first time and had to be there before 12:00 midnight before she went to bed. At least that's what she told him. Since it was only 7:00 p.m., he thought he would have time to see his friends, the three bears. They lived in three different houses. One bear lived in a straw house, another in a stick house, and the last bear lived in a brick house. Suddenly, he heard crunching under the carriage wheels. "What the…?" he said, confused. He looked down and saw that his beautiful long hair was caught in the wheels. The carriage went out of control. "Why won't this carriage turn?!" he yelled. Then he found himself heading straight into one of the bears' houses! "Look out!" the giant shouted to the bears. Finally, he got the carriage to stop right before hitting the houses. "Ah-choo!" The giant turned around and saw his seven brothers, hiding in the back of the carriage. "Sneezy! You blew our cover! And more importantly, you ruined the bears' houses with your sneezing!"

"What are you guys doing here?!" the giant said.

"We wanted to come along with you to grandmother's house," Dopey said.

The giant looked at what used to be the bears' houses. "Oh, my gosh!" the giant gasped. The bears were devastated. Sneezy got out of the carriage to apologize to the bears.

"I'm so sorry!" Sneezy said. "Can I help you rebuild your houses?"

"It's okay," the bears said, sadly. "We can rebuild them."

The giant had just noticed all the rubble they were standing in. "I'm really sorry about them. They snuck into my carriage!"

"Don't worry about it. We wanted to redo our houses, anyway." Papa Bear said.

"Oh, good," the giant said, relieved. He looked at his watch. It was almost 10 p.m.! "Oh, no! We have only two hours to get to grandmother's house! We have to hurry!"

"Don't worry. We'll help you," the dwarves said.

Since the pumpkin carriage had been destroyed, the giant and the dwarves had to walk the rest of the way. "Bye, bears!" shouted the giant.

"Bye! See you later!" the bears shouted back. "We hope you get to your grandmother's house safely!"

"Thank you! Bye!"

The giant and his dwarf brothers walked for almost an hour. "Come on! You guys can get on my back, and we can run the rest of the way," the tired giant said.

"Oh, yeah. We'd better hurry," Grumpy said. The giant picked up all the dwarves, put them on his back, and started running. The whole forest appeared to shake as the giant thumped his huge feet across the forest floor. They were almost there when Dopey smelled something good.

"What's that delicious smell?" he asked.

"I think it's gingerbread," the giant said.

"Is that grandmother's house?" Doc asked.

"This is the place," said the giant.

"Yay!" said Happy.

All the dwarves climbed off the giant's back. Dopey ran up to the house and peered into the window. He screamed and ran straight back to the group. He'd seen an ugly witch. She had a long, green nose with pimples on it and long, dark, straggly hair hanging in front of her ugly face. She was straightening her torn black dress and stirring stew in a big pot. At first, Dopey did not realize the witch was his grandmother. Then, all the dwarves started running around wildly until the giant

Mini-Me (My Children and Grandchildren)

told them to be quiet. "Shhhh!" said the giant. "I can't believe my grandmother's a witch!" He was angry. Because he was too big to fit in the house, he told the dwarves to sneak into the house and try to capture her. It didn't work out so well.

"HAAHAAHAA!" the witch cackled. "That's right! Come into my house!" (code name for "trap"). When she came out of her house, she had all the dwarves tied up by their feet. She was using her magic wand to make them float.

"Help!" all the dwarves shouted to the giant.

"Wow! You've grown so tall! HAAAAHAAAHAA!" the witch laughed. "How about we give you some stew to help you grow more? Don't be shy!"

But the giant didn't listen to her. Then, he took off one of his glass slippers and smashed it on the ground. The witch was confused.

"What are you doing?" she said to him.

Finally, he was finished. "Yes! I'm done!" He gathered all his long hair and chopped it off with the sharpest piece of glass from his slipper that he could find. The hair fell to the ground into a large pile. He picked it up and started to swing it in the air.

The dwarves realized what the giant was doing and cheered quietly.

"Wait — what are you doing with that?" The witch started to back away.

The giant's hair was whipping around so fast that there was a great wind that blew through the trees and smashed the witch's house into pieces. The witch was furious!

"Look at what you've done to my house! You ruined it!"

The witch threw the dwarves back onto the ground with her wand.

"Hey! Ow!" the dwarves cried.

"Don't you dare hurt them!" the giant said.

Then he lassoed the witch and spun her around rapidly. "I've got you now!" he said. With his super giant strength, he flung the witch far into the forest for good.

"AAAAAHHHHH!" the witch screamed. That was the last anyone ever heard of the fake granny.

"Bye, bye, mean old witch!" Grumpy cheered.

"You saved us!" Bashful blushed.

"Hooray for the giant!" the dwarves sang.

Then they all skipped along back home. The giant had saved everybody.

"I'm so glad no one will ever have to deal with her again," the giant said.

Then they all celebrated with porridge and lived happily ever after!

The End!

By Gabriella Gorka (Age 11)

Contributions by Sophia and Domenick Gorka

Mini-Me (My Children and Grandchildren)

Notes to Grandchildren

1. You are here to learn, conquer yourself, help others, and make God smile.

2. Friends move away. Family is with you your entire life.

3. The closer you get to your potential, the more successful and happier you are.

4. Strive to be the best version of yourself.

5. Attitude is everything. With every day and every action, you have a choice.

6. It is not what happens to you that's important — it is how you react to it.

7. We are spiritual beings, temporarily living in a physical body. "Your body gets older, but your spirit stays at age 18." — Dad

8. Try not to do or say anything you will regret.

9. Live the Ten Commandments. "What will it profit a man if he gains the whole world, yet forfeits his soul?" Matthew 16:26

10. Don't ignore the connection between food and health.

11. Don't ignore the connection between spirituality and happiness.

12. Whether you think you can or you can't, you're right.

Me for Thee (My Philosophy and My Legacy)

Family Story Book

One of the most rewarding experiences for me occurred in 2002. There were some stories I had written to pass on to my children and grandchildren. I was certain there were other members of my family who also had stories to preserve. I sent out a letter to all my aunts and uncles on both sides of my family, asking them to submit their story for a Family Story Book. If they preferred, they could send me a tape, and I would transcribe it. My father's side of the family accepted my offer with great enthusiasm. Even my Uncle Joe, who'd been at Iwo Jima and had never discussed his experience, was willing to share his story with us. My mother's side of the family did not appear interested. No stories, so no book for them. My father took movies of everything. With a little bit of work and tons of editing, I assembled movies of all my aunts and uncles from their childhood up into their 80s. There were three components to my project: 1) a DVD with film clips of all my aunts and uncles as they grew 2) a seven-generation family tree and 3) all the stories that had been submitted. The project was a tremendous hit. When Mom's memory began to fail, I would read hers and my father's stories to her. Her eyes would light up as she listened, and she would always say, "How do you know this?" I would reply, "These are the stories you and Dad wrote when you were younger." She loved them, as did the entire family. The side effect of the Family Story Book was that I became more interested in writing stories; hence this book.

Traditions

Family Vacations

Almost every Sunday, we would get together with Daria, Tara, and their families at one of our houses for dinner, discussion, games, or planning a family trip. There would be one significant

Turks and Caicos

Me for Thee (My Philosophy and My Legacy)

family vacation each year that we all attended — Long Beach Island, Disney, and Turks and Caicos Islands. At Long Beach Island, Gabriella and I would run toward each other and jump into the air, hoping to meet in the middle and "high-five" each other, while Daria tried to capture that perfect moment with a photo. The photo below was our 15th attempt. There are phones and cameras now that can capture every photo in the sequence, doing away with the need for multiple tries. It's about time. I am still out of breath.

Bob and Gabriella Flying at Long Beach Island

Italy
Parma

Italy holds a very special place in our family's hearts. We have made six or seven trips there. Our first trip was in 1984, when Savia's parents announced that they would take all of us to Italy.

A Blessed and Guided Life

Mama left Italy when she was 14, and this trip was 50 years later. The first thing that strikes you in Italy is how old the buildings are. There are few trees in Italy, so everything is made of stone, marble, and concrete. It is built to last, and it does. The Colosseum was built around 70 AD and still has many areas intact. Another thing that I wasn't expecting was the unusual preparation for renovating buildings. When the exterior of a building is being repaired, a drop cloth would be hung over that area. The drop cloth is embroidered with the image of the original building. This resulted in a beautiful building — even if it was being repaired.

Don't ever mistake gelato for ice cream. After eating one ice cream, your stomach knows you've had enough. But you can eat gelato three, four, or five times a day without any ill effects — and we did.

The food in northern Italy is permeated with light and white sauces, while the food in southern Italy is mainly composed of red sauces. If you are not sure which part of Italy you are in, you could use the food as your latitudinal map.

We arrived at night and had difficulty finding our hotel in Parma, so we asked for directions. We were told to go to Semaforo, take a left, and go two blocks. We drove round and round but couldn't find a street sign with that name. Eventually, we asked someone else, who said *"semaforo"* meant "traffic light." Knowing that made directions a whole lot easier.

The first relatives we visited were in Parma, in the northern part of Italy. I was the only adult who did not speak Italian, so I mostly sat in the corner, waiting for my cue. Savia taught me to say *"mi piace il cibo,"* which means "I like the food." When my big moment presented itself, I shined. Then my light went out, and I was relegated back to mannequin status.

Me for Thee (My Philosophy and My Legacy)

Another set of relatives lived on a farm in Dongola, near Parma. One of the gifts we brought with us from America was a necktie. When we presented this to our cousin Giovanni, we were not sure what his facial expression meant. It seems that not only did he not wear a necktie, he didn't know what it was. Should he use it to pull the cows? To colorfully wrap an injured arm? Such was the puzzlement on his face.

We saw the stone building where Savia's great-grandfather and grandfather were born and the more-modern stone outdoor bathroom with running water. Savia's father still owns a portion of the land, but the earthquakes and landslides make the actual location difficult to determine. The relatives tried to give us an idea of where his portion of the property was. We walked through the grassy hills constantly waving a stick in front of us to scare away any hidden snakes.

During certain times of the year, there is a fairly large river that had to be crossed to reach the property. Savia's grandfather would walk on stilts to cross. Fortunately, a bridge was built to make the trip easier, however, the bridge sometimes gets washed out, and the stilts are often used until repairs are made.

Many relatives heard that the Americans were coming to the farmhouse to visit, so they joined us, however, the relatives spoke only Italian. After growing up around the language my whole life, I did understand some words. They said not to worry. George would arrive shortly from England, and I could speak with him. When George finally did arrive, his cockney English accent made him more unintelligible than the Italians. Back to mannequin status.

During our trip, my arm and legs felt a little itchy. As time went on, the intensity increased, and blotches formed. I suspected measles and was not sure if I'd had that as a child. I had to relieve the itching but knew that scratching it would spread the problem. My solution was to carry a magazine around and hit myself with it instead of scratching. Imagine seeing someone waiting at a bus stop, frequently slapping themselves with a magazine. It did relieve the symptoms somewhat, but it was a strange sight to an observer. I didn't care. Our next thought was that, if I did indeed have measles, I would be quarantined until it was over, along with the rest of my family. The solution was for me to stay in the hotel room while everyone else went sightseeing. For a few days, I heard the stories of what amazing sights I had missed, but the itching got worse. I finally gave in and asked the hotel for a doctor.

About 20 minutes later, a doctor came to my room to examine me. A large portion of my arms and legs was filled with lavender-red blotches. After the doctor examined me, he said he would like to bring me to the hospital for another opinion. Savia and I squeezed into his little Fiat, and we drove at hair-raising speed (good — I could use more hair) around the twisting, curving roads to the hospital in Bologna. Upon entering the hospital, I sat on a bench in a large, dimly lit entrance, with ceilings at least 20 feet high. I could see sunlight through the enormous front doors, which had remained open. We waited while the doctor went to assemble some of his associates. About 15 minutes later, four additional doctors came to examine me, one carrying an oversized reference manual. After a careful exam and paging through the reference manual, they decided it was the worst case they had ever seen of "poison grass," a type of poison ivy. It wasn't until then that I remembered pruning rose bushes on the perimeter of my house in New Jersey before I left, so that it wouldn't be waiting for me after vacation — a mistake. They prescribed an ointment to be used daily and gave me an injection. The doctor then drove us back to the hotel at the same speed as before. The cost of having the doctor come to the hotel, bring me to the hospital, consult with his associates, give me the ointment and injection, and driving me back was $10.

Sicily

On the next phase of our trip, we visited Savia's relatives in Sicily. We rented a car at the airport in Catania. The rental agent cautioned us about tying the luggage to the roof of the car. It seems that, at stop lights, the luggage might be removed by everyday, common thieves, which sometimes includes children. We took that advice. At one point, we noticed that a car had difficulty finding a place to park, so the two men got out of their car, picked up a small Fiat, and moved it out of "their" space. We drove to Lingualosa, where the Emmi family lives, but we did not know the exact house number. So we asked someone where Sal Emmi lived, and he said that *all* the males there were named Sal Emmi. However, he knew we were from America and were looking for the one called "Joe," who was expecting us. The families discussed their common ancestry while all the children played together. It was a wonderful reunion.

    I found it interesting that, in the same manner our house gutters become filled with leaves, at Sal Emmi's house, their gutters become filled with volcanic ash. Everyone looked a little ash-covered being that they were near Mt. Etna. That night, they insisted we stay at their house, and we did. It was very welcoming but hot, since there was no air conditioning, and quarters were tight. The next morning, we had breakfast together and spent the day visiting where Mama's house was located and many other wonderful sights. However, we mentioned that we needed to get a hotel so we could be more comfortable. We left and made reservations at the Holiday Inn in Catania, not far from Linguaglosa. We spent a few days with Mama's relatives, going to see the volcano on Mount Etna and to a parade in town. The group that was performing at the time was from Yugoslavia. We had such a good time together, but it was time to get back to the U.S.

Years later, on another trip to Sicily, we drove to our hotel in Taormina, on the top of a mountain. The area had a tropical climate, with amazing scenery and crystal blue water. Access to the beach was through an elevator that had been dug out of the center of the mountain. Once you reach the bottom, you're in a large, lighted cave about a 100-yard walk from the rocky beach.

One thousand feet above our hotel in Taormina is a town called Castelmola. It is a town above a town. This is where we wanted to have dinner. It was a 20 minute drive up a steep, four-mile, spiral-staircase-type road to the restaurant at the summit. We were at a corner table overlooking the landscape and ocean below, with metal fencing on the side of our table with stringlights along the top. It was dark when the waiter came to take our dinner order, and he noticed a bulb was out. He proceeded to climb to the top of the metal fence — a 1,000-foot drop to the town below. We all shouted, "No! Not now! Change it later!" Dinner was fine, with a great view.

Traveling Salesman
Bruges, Belgium

Tara was dating Jud, a boy in high school. His family was originally from Alabama and Mississippi, but because his father worked at Exxon, they were able to travel and live all over the world. Jack and Gwen, Jud's parents, heard that we did retirement planning and investments, a service they were interested in. We started the process when they unexpectedly

Me for Thee (My Philosophy and My Legacy)

were transferred to Bruges, Belgium. They asked if we wanted to continue our discussion in Bruges and spend Christmas week with them. We accepted. When we arrived in Bruges several weeks later, we discovered that all the sidewalks were damp and covered with moss — which, for all we knew, was common at that time of the year. The city was still very picturesque — "The Venice of the North." During our visit, we did some sightseeing. One of the most memorable sights was the Basilica of the Holy Blood in Bruges, which contains a relic said to have been brought there around 1150 AD during the Second Crusade and is supposed to be a cloth with the blood of Christ preserved by Joseph of Arimathea after he washed the dead body of Christ. The blood has not coagulated after all these years. I was not aware of this relic until our trip.

We also took a one-day side trip to Paris, at which time we saw the Eiffel Tower. I realize it is recognized as a beautiful structure, however, with all its girders and bolts visible, to me it looked like an unfinished building or a skeletal, unclothed version of the Empire State Building. It took me several days to be able to properly pronounce the main street in Paris, Champs-Élysées.

At night, we would watch TV or talk. Jack and Gwen were fond of alcoholic beverages during dinner, which is not uncommon, except for my family, who rarely drink. Christmas Day was approaching, and Gwen announced that we would be having lasagna. She went to the supermarket with Savia to buy the ingredients. Savia assumed that, being Italian, Gwen would rely on her to either make or assist with preparing the lasagna. That assumption was incorrect. Gwen bought the pasta and cottage cheese she thought she needed. I don't think I have ever had cottage cheese, but to use it in lasagna was blasphemous to an Italian. Gwen prepared the entire dinner without assistance, and I am surprised to report that it was actually good, including the side dish of black-eyed peas, Gwen being from Mississippi and all. There is always something new to learn. We spent a wonderful week with them and enjoyed getting to know each other and sightseeing.

We were back at home in New Jersey when it was our turn to show Jack and Gwen our hospitality. They were in town for a few days, so we invited them to stay at our house to reciprocate. They were very pleasant, sociable people. The next morning, I went downstairs and noticed that the liquor cabinet was open. We rarely open that cabinet, since we rarely drink liquor. How could that have happened? Did Jack or Gwen come down for a nightcap? Do we ask them about it? Was there some other explanation? We decided to ignore it.

The next day, our frisky, young Persian cats, Raja and Sheba, were playing when Raja jumped onto the countertop over the liquor cabinet. On her way down, her feet pressed on the spring-loaded door and opened it.

Hopefully, we learned not to assume or judge, a nasty human habit.

Bedtime Lullaby

It all started when we had our first child, Daria. Savia would rock Daria to sleep singing a lullaby she'd made up and named "My Little Horsey." Then when Tara came along, she too, was rocked to sleep with the lullaby. As the girls got older, this became our bedtime ritual, along with a prayer before going to sleep. Now both Daria and Tara continue to sing this to their children at bedtime.

Savia singing "My Little Horsey — Gabriella & Sophia — *https://www.youtube.com/watch?v=OxPPlqwKtj8* and "My Little Horsey — Siena" — *https://www.youtube.com/watch?v=I5qzMuzReZI*

Me for Thee (My Philosophy and My Legacy)

My Little Horsey
July 1977
Savia Giarraffa

Transcribed by Bruce Gatewood

A Blessed and Guided Life

Easter Egg Hunt

Each year at Easter, I would design an Easter Egg Hunt, known as "The Hunt." The first one took place while we were still at Sanford Drive in 1985. Savia's parents and my parents participated, along with our brothers and sisters. Occasionally, friends would join us. I would arrange teams whose goal was to solve a riddle which would lead them to the next clue until, after about 12 to 15 clues, they would arrive at a plastic Easter egg filled with chocolates.

Savia, Gabriella, Dario, Michele, Sophia and Daria

Me for Thee (My Philosophy and My Legacy)

*Pasquale, Cesare, Tara, Domenick, Gregory,
Gabriella, Daria, Erik and Sophia*

Some years The Hunt would be at my house, and other years, it would be at one of the local parks or down at our community lake. One year, I sent out a pre-hunt survey asking each participant what level of difficulty they wanted. Savia's brother indicated "very difficult." I had him wading in a lake, ducking branches to find his clues. Another year, when The Hunt was at Hedden Park, the clue was Kids Volley Kids 97 Jerks. Dario and his team could not solve the riddle, so they asked if they were warm or cold, meaning close or far from the clue. I indicated "warm," because they were standing next to the clue but didn't see it. Then someone else needed my help about 50 yards down the street, so I got into my car and drove there. Dario and his team were standing in the same spot as before when I changed my indicator to "cold." This *really* confused them. The clue was the license plate on my car ("KVK97J"), which was now in motion. Another clue was in a rock-filled sterno can, hung from a string off the side of a bridge.

Loretta's daughter, Andrea, recently told me that she has hosted Easter Egg Hunts like the ones she participated in at my house. You may not be aware of how your actions affect others and how they affect you. We are all connected.

Seating Arrangements

Dario's wife, Michele, and I have special seating arrangements at meals. Dario started dating Michele and would come along with Savia's parents when they visited us at Sanford Drive on Sundays. Everyone was speaking Italian, and Michele and I could not and did not join in the conversation. So, instead of talking across and around other people, we decided to sit next to each other, so we had someone to talk to. There has not been a meal that we were both at where we did not sit together. It has been 37 years and counting.

Making Struffoli

Each year, around Christmas, Mom and two of her sisters, Aunt Rose and Aunt Jo, would get together and make an Italian dessert called *struffoli*. It was an arduous, daylong process requiring a dedicated team of people, each with their own job in the assembly-line preparation, which turned the kitchen into something resembling a FEMA rescue area. This tradition continues and has spread through her and her sisters' families and their childrens'. One year, we videotaped Mom while she talked us through this involved process.

Me for Thee (My Philosophy and My Legacy)

Link to Nanny making Struffoli: *https://youtu.be/RCfD1v1-QQI*

Robert, Tara, Savia, Pasquale, Erik, Daria and Domenick

Struffoli Recipe

Makes 1 batch = 24 struffoli cups

Ingredients:

Struffoli patties:
- 2½ cups flour
- ¼ cup sugar
- 1 teaspoon vanilla extract
- 4 large eggs
- 1 large tablespoon butter (room temperature)
- 2 teaspoons baking powder

Honey Mixture:
- Pure canola oil
- ¼ cup honey
- ⅛ cup water
- 2 tablespoons sugar
- 8 oz. slivered almonds
- Rainbow nonpareils

Struffoli Dough:
Combine baking powder and flour. Create a well.
Combine sugar and butter in well.
Beat eggs in bowl.
Slowly add eggs into well, and combine with sugar and butter.
Gradually incorporate flour into the egg/flour/butter mixture.
Once dough begins to form/solidify, knead dough with hands.
Slice dough down the center to look for bubbles. When bubbles are present, the dough is complete.
Run dough through pasta maker at widest setting to flatten.
Then form strips (like linguine) with pasta maker.
Cut dough into small balls, and set aside.

Struffoli Frying:
Heat oil in deep fryer to 400°.
Place dough balls in fryer. Remove dough when it rises to the top and is slightly browned.
Strain dough, and place in a paper bag.

Slightly dampen countertop or work surface with cool water.

Honey Coating:
In a frying pan, combine honey, water, sugar, and slivered almonds.
Turn mixture over medium heat until it completely bubbles.
Add struffoli to the pan and combine mixture until thin strings form throughout the pan.

Place struffoli/honey mixture on countertop, and form patties.
Sprinkle nonpareils on patties while they are warm.

Let patties cool, and place them in cupcake holders.

Ending

I was blessed to be born in the United States, in Brooklyn, to wonderful parents and relatives.

I don't think it was a coincidence that I survived a very premature birth in 1947, when infant mortality rates were much higher than today.

I don't think it was a coincidence that I attended one of the best high schools in the country.

I don't think it was a coincidence that I missed the policeman's exam to later become a Financial Advisor.

I don't think it was a coincidence that I failed chemistry and then majored in chemistry and was introduced to Savia as a thank-you for helping my cousin pass *his* chemistry exam.

I don't think it was a coincidence that I dated someone else for five years but married Savia.

I don't think it was a coincidence that Savia's parents were a model and prelude to self-employment.

I don't think it was a coincidence that I went to Connecticut to find a job in New Jersey.

I don't think it was a coincidence that Savia had investments before we were married that ignited my interest in investing and financial planning.

I don't think it was a coincidence that I was introduced to Tomorrow's Financial Services, who gave me a template to succeed.

I don't think it was a coincidence that I survived the health issues of my thirties to start a new career that helped people.

I don't think it was a coincidence that Barbara and Joe came to work for me when I needed help.

A Blessed and Guided Life

There is a movie called *The Adjustment Bureau*, in which we find a person who was born with a life plan. Anytime the person deviated from the plan, The Adjustment Bureau would intervene, without his knowledge, to get him back on track.

I consider these "coincidences" intelligent dominos that led me to a happy, fulfilled life, enabling me to use the talents and skills I was given.

I have truly been blessed.

Me for Thee (My Philosophy and My Legacy)

When Gabriella was looking through the pictures of our Disney World trip on my phone, she came across a picture of a gravestone with the name "Giarraffa" on it. She asked who it was for. I replied, "For Nana and me." I told her that we didn't want to leave the task of choosing the stone to someone else. *What if we didn't like it?*

When you are in the neighborhood, stop by and visit. I am with my wife, Savia, at Pleasant Grove Cemetery in Chester, New Jersey, by the main entrance.

Acknowledgments

My wife, Savia, was the first to review each story for grammar and content while the ink was still drying. The recollection of the events may not have been accurate, and it was great to have a memory check during the book writing.

The next step in the process was an additional grammar, memory check, and social etiquette review by my daughter, Daria. You must keep up with the current phraseology.

My daughter, Tara, is the Ultimate Editor. After the editor and I reviewed the manuscript, Tara suggested about 300 additional improvements. I am not sure where she obtained this ability from, but there is no doubt she has it.

My son-in-law Erik transformed my videos into links to bring action to some of the sections.

Bruce Gatewood, my guitar teacher, converted Savia's bedtime lullaby into actual sheet music so anyone can play it. It took hours watching clips of Savia singing. But in the end, an in-person interview was needed.

Thanks to my "Work Family", Joe Okaly, Barbara Ricciardi, James Barron, Kim Matlock and Jess Chowdhury, who endured my stories as I spoon-fed them one at a time.

After each story that I shared with Kathryn Korin, she would call me excitedly to discuss the details and background story.

Thanks to Donna J. Atkins, The Life Story Lady, who provided the format, Pre-Me, Becoming Me, etc., that I learned at her Life Story Workshop, which solved the perennial timeline issues involved in autobiographies.

To the many people who found joy in my stories and encouraged me to continue writing including Bernie Tuosto, Drs. Matt and Meagan McGowan, Greg Kemp, Helen Lippman, Diane Okaly, Jim Basso, Jon Hauge, Mary Matullo, Don and Madeline McDermott, Nicole Olivo, Nicole Przybylko, Dario and Michele Manfredi, Ralph Castriotta, Dr. Francis McGovern, and Vinny Faviano.

Thanks also to Michele, the owner of 1106 Design, who made me think that publishing my book was possible and to Brian, Frank, and Ronda, who walked me through each step of the book-design process.

About the Author

Born and raised in Brooklyn, New York, Robert Giarraffa attended St. John's University in Queens, NY, graduating in 1968 with a Bachelor's Degree in Chemistry. He began his career in the pharmaceutical industry where he worked for 15 years. Robert was  concurrently a member of the Army National Guard from 1969 to 1976. He went on to attend Fairleigh Dickinson University, graduating in 1976 with an MBA in Finance.

Robert began his career in the financial industry as a Financial Advisor in 1978. He went on to found New Horizons in 1982. As President of New Horizons Wealth Management LLC, he trains and manages other financial advisors. In 1993, he created Backdoor Budgeting^{SM}, a Federally Registered method used to analyze cash flow. He has been a member of the Financial Planning Association (formerly the International Association for Financial Planners) since 1983.

Robert sponsors and plays on the New Horizons Wealth Management LLC softball team having done so since 1997.

He enjoys playing ping-pong and pool, as well as designing Microsoft Excel programs and reading non-fiction books. Robert enjoys traveling and is an advocate of complementary medicine. In his hometown, he was a member of the Randolph Open Space Committee from 1999 to 2007.

Robert has lived with his wife, Savia, in Randolph, New Jersey since 1973 with daughters, Daria & Tara living close by with their families in Madison, New Jersey.

www.ingramcontent.com/pod-product-compliance
Lightning Source LLC
Chambersburg PA
CBHW042124100526
44587CB00026B/4172